HOW TO RUN
A SUCCESSFUL
RESTAURANT

The Small Business Series

DAVID M. BROWNSTONE, *GENERAL EDITOR*

HOW TO RUN A SUCCESSFUL RESTAURANT

William L. Siegel

A HUDSON GROUP BOOK

DAVID M. BROWNSTONE, *General Editor*

John Wiley & Sons, Inc.
New York • Chichester • Brisbane • Toronto • Singapore

Library of Congress Cataloging in Publication Data

Siegel, William Laird.
How to run a successful restaurant.

(Wiley small business series)
Includes index.

1. Restaurant management. I. Title.
TX911.3.M27S53   1980   658'.91'64795   79-25240
ISBN 0-471-07910-3

12   13   14   15   16   17   18   19   20

CONTENTS

PART ONE

Running Your Restaurant

ONE

You and
Your Restaurant

Advantages and Drawbacks to Owning a Restaurant / A Typical Day in a Small Restaurant / Is It for You? / SBA Checklist

ADVANTAGES AND DRAWBACKS TO OWNING A RESTAURANT

RESTAURANTS ARE EVERYWHERE. THEY COME IN ALL SHAPES, sizes, and national origins. In large cities like New York and San Francisco you can literally eat in a different restaurant each night for years. But restaurants have not nearly reached their saturation point. The American public is still ready, willing, and able to spend more millions in new restaurants.

So if you own a restaurant now or are planning to open one in the near (or far) future, you won't see the bottom drop out of the business suddenly and savagely. People need to eat, and they will continue to need to eat.

But the restaurant business is far from ideal for the starry-eyed individual who just wants to start his or her own business. The mortality rate of new restaurants is appalling. Half fail or change management every five years. Most banks refuse to consider substantial loans to new restaurateurs, because they are such bad risks.

The big question is, Why? Unlike any other small business, restaurants are considered easy by novices. Any housewife who throws a successful luau, or possibly her husband, who can grill six steaks to perfection on the barbecue, thinks he or she possesses all the talent needed to open a restaurant. Well, it just ain't so. The restaurant business is full of people who spend their hard-earned money without really digging into the ins and outs of the business and then lose their shirts.

It may be heresy to some people, but the businessman or businesswoman must consider potential profits and how difficult it is to make those profits. That charming old Victorian house out in the back woods of Maine may make a splendid inn—except for the fact that it is located forty miles from any highway on a small dirt road that is snowbound for most of the winter. But chances are some poor soul will buy it and attempt to make a restaurant out of it.

The restaurant business has many sides; cooking is only a part of the business activities. The owner must know how to purchase, store, advertise, keep accurate records, analyze sales figures, handle employees, keep customers happy, and a thousand other things. Sure, some people blunder along, surviving year after year by the grace of God. But the vast majority of new restaurant owners who are not well prepared just sink out of sight after a year or two. Take a trip through any good-sized town. Look at the restaurants. How many of them have been successful for a number of years? And how many regularly send up those "under new management" banners, or shut down altogether?

Yet the restaurant business has so much to offer people who go into it with both eyes open. The satisfaction can be immense. Creative, vital innovators can carve a real niche for themselves in the business. Gourmets can preserve their recipes and make history with culinary achievements. Businessmen can go wild thinking up new ways to attract customers or planning efficiency programs that will cut costs and increase profits.

This book isn't meant to be a complete outline of success. There just isn't such a beast. The best-laid plans of mice and men gang aft agley—Robert Burns probably had a local inn in mind when he penned that quotation. But if you carefully read this book, you'll have a good idea of what to expect. The book is for both novices and current restaurant owners who may be wondering what they did wrong—or what they did right.

The guiding theme of this book is awareness. That's the key. Know what you're doing before it becomes a *fait accompli*. The better you understand your business, the less likely that you'll get nasty surprises.

A TYPICAL DAY IN A SMALL RESTAURANT

It is five in the morning. Sal and Sandy have just opened the door of their small diner located on a bay in the Florida Keys. It overlooks the aqua water of the Gulf of Mexico. Every few minutes seem to bring in more and more laughing, joking fishermen who order steaming coffee and plates of cold key lime pie.

By six the diner is bustling with activity. Sal can hardly keep up with demand for bacon and eggs. By eleven the last friendly fisherman has left, and Sal and Sandy's day is finished. They close the door, pull down the shades, and head off to the beach to lie in the sun.

Sounds good, doesn't it? Occasionally, running a restaurant can be like this, but it won't be the most successful business in the country. You see, Sal owns an apartment building in St. Louis and also has a retirement pension. He can afford to lie in the sun! If a small restaurant is your only business, and provides you with your only source of income, then the overwhelming probability is that you will work long hours in order to make your business succeed. The plain truth is that running any business, especially a restaurant, is a full-time, tough, demanding job. And the sad reality is that the restaurant business is full of people who have decided on the spur of the moment that they can run a restaurant. They jump in with their eyes closed and their pockets open, and before you know it, another restaurant has bitten the dust.

Yes, running a restaurant can be difficult, but there are also advantages. You are your own boss. You can have the unique satisfaction of watching something you create flower and grow. And, of course, you can claim the success that you have earned —if and when you earn it.

If you are serious about starting a restaurant, take a look at how a typical small restaurant is run. A good example is Ed's Rockwood Diner. It's located in the center of a medium-sized suburb of New York City. Ed reaches his place by six each morning, before any other employee, the first to arrive and the last to leave. The first thing he does is a little cleaning up from the night before, when he was too beat to face it. Since breakfast is the first meal, Ed prepares batter for pancakes and mixes the eggs and milk for the french toast. He checks the supply of eggs, bacon, and bread and starts the coffee perking.

Molly, the morning waitress, pops in at five to seven, just five minutes before the doors open for business and ten minutes after she is due. She rushes around, trying to get into her uniform and organize the menus at the same time.

Ed sighs and goes back to preparing the coffee. The last time he yelled at Molly for being late she broke into tears and didn't work the rest of the day. Ed shakes his head as he remembers having to cook, wait on customers, and console Molly all at the same time. He wants no more of that.

At ten after seven, a small group of local businessmen drift in. Ed waves to them and they joke back and forth. He knows by heart exactly what each one will order. They come back day after day, so Ed makes sure they get extra special attention and a big hello.

By eight o'clock the diner is hopping. Ed is too busy scrambling eggs and frying bacon to joke any more. He understands that most of his customers have little time for anything except a quick bite and a cup of coffee. Many are late for work as it is.

The sound of breaking glass and a scream from Molly rivet Ed's attention. Fearing the worst, he glances up from his grill. Luckily it was only a small juice glass, and a friendly customer is apologizing to Molly for being clumsy. Last week Molly dropped a tray on someone who wasn't so understanding. It took fifteen precious minutes during rush hour to calm him down. A free breakfast finally did the trick.

By nine the rush is over, and Ed turns to preparing for lunch —shredding lettuce, slicing tomatoes, and mixing the cold beverages. His wife, June, comes in at ten. They have two school-age children, so June takes over the cash register, helps purchase the supplies, and does a little bookkeeping until late afternoon when the children get home.

Business is light for the next hour and a half. Ed and June

take advantage of the break to go over their finances. June points out how they are losing lunch business to a new fast-food chain that recently opened up across the street. Ed sugfests they start a salad bar and print up a new, more stylish menu to draw in more customers. June agrees and adds that they should take out some advertising in the local newspaper.

At eleven-thirty the first luncheon customers arrive and everyone goes back to work. Ed has calculated the number of hamburger patties and hot dogs needed for the rush, and they are waiting in the refrigerator, ready for quick use.

Ed is glad to see many of the same faces that had been in the diner for breakfast. He is proud that many of his regular customers have not deserted him for the new fried-chicken restaurant. But still, there are empty seats that weren't there before the competition opened its doors. Ed starts to think seriously about the new salad bar.

As Ed grills a medium-rare burger, he watches the lemonade container a little uneasily. The day turned out hotter than expected, and there was a run on the cold drinks. Unfortunately, that is the last of the lemonade, and the delivery man isn't expected until two o'clock tomorrow. As it nears the bottom, Ed thinks fast. He lowers the price of the orange drink, putting it up as a blackboard special. Customers switch, and the day is saved.

At two o'clock the lunch rush is over. Business is good, and the busier it is, the better Ed likes it. At two thirty some high school students come in to take their jobs as dishwasher and bus boys. Ed enjoys working with them and helps them along as much as possible. In return, they are highly reliable.

Between two and four dinner is prepared. Ed puts rolls and pies in to bake, makes a huge pot of split-pea soup as the soup du jour, and checks his stock of steak and chops.

Molly and June have left and have been replaced by Steve and Alice. Both wait on tables, but Ed has been training Steve to do some cooking as well. Ed plans to have Steve take over all the dinner cooking someday in order that Ed can spend more time at home with his family. Ed hopes to expand and hire enough help so that he can become the restaurant's full-time manager. But that's in the future. Right now he has to make sure the grill is set properly and everything is ready for the evening shift.

At a quarter to six the customers start arriving. The advertised special for the night is New York strip steak, so Ed is expecting a heavy crowd. He has prepared his supplies to meet the demand.

As expected, customers pour in. With Steve's help the cooking goes smoothly. By nine o'clock Ed is both exhausted and pleased. The day's turnover was high, there was only one complaint—from a woman who had ordered a medium-well steak and decided she had gotten a medium-rare one. There were a few compliments. Steve and Alice were also happy, since tips on steak night are generally higher than usual.

The last customer is out by ten o'clock. The dishwashers have left by nine thirty. Ed takes a look around, straightens up a little, then decides he'll come in early tomorrow to finish the cleaning. He's beat. At ten twenty Ed leaves for home, two blocks away.

So there you have a brief look at what running a restaurant is all about, multiplied by six or seven days a week. Of course, many small-restaurant owners use different procedures. There are dozens of different types of eating establishments. But in general, Ed is a typical small-restaurant owner. He is involved with every detail of running his restaurant. He orders supplies, he cooks, he manages, he hires and fires the employees, he worries about competition, and he plans for the future. He alternates between worrying about lemonade and planning how his restaurant can compete with a fast-food chain.

IS IT FOR YOU?

There is good and bad in running a small restaurant. Whether it's for you depends on what you want. You must be able to do everything. When a waitress is ill, you wait on tables. If a cook is out, you become the chef. It can be a pain or a plus, you can love it or loathe it. It can be a source of immense gratification and a profitable venture or a nightmare leading to bankruptcy.

Are you the right type of person to run a small restaurant?

This is an important question to consider. As you can see from Ed's example, running a restaurant properly takes a special type of individual. First, you must know how to prepare meals. Second, you must get along with people, both customers and employees. Third, you have to have common business sense. The third criterion is relatively easy to discover about yourself. You may know how to cook for five, but how about fifty? And you may think you can get along with people, until a major crisis occurs and *both* customers and employees are yelling at you. On-the-job experience will prove whether or not you can take it. But the business aspects of running a restaurant can be predetermined.

The Small Business Administration provides a number of penetrating questions for the novice going into any small business. Take a look at them. If you are starting out, the questions will tell you a great deal about your chances for success. Even if you have operated a small restaurant for years, look at the questions as though you were going into business tomorrow. See if you did the right things when you began.

BEFORE YOU START

How about YOU?

Are you the kind of person who can get a business started and make it go?

Think about why you want to own your own business. Do you want to badly enough to keep you working long hours without knowing how much money you'll end up with?

Have you worked in a business like the one you want to start?

Have you worked for someone else as a foreman or manager?

Have you had any business training in school?

Have you saved any money?

How about the money?

Do you know how much money you will need to get your business started?

Have you counted up how much money of your own you can put into the business?

Do you know how much credit you can get from your suppliers, the people you will buy from?

Do you know where you can borrow the rest of the money you need to start your own business?

Have you figured out what net income per year you expect to get from the business? Count your salary and your profit on the money you put into the business.

Can you live on less than this so that you can use some of it to help your business grow?

Have you talked to a banker about your plans?

How about a partner?

If you need a partner with money or know-how that you don't have, do you know someone who will fit, someone you can get along with?

Do you know the good and bad points about going it alone, having a partner, and incorporating your business?

Have you talked to a lawyer about it?

How about your customers?

Do most of the businesses in your community seem to be doing well?

Have you tried to find out whether operations like the one you want to open are doing well in your community and in the rest of the country?

Do you know what kind of people will want to buy what you plan to sell?

Do people like that live in the area where you want to open your restaurant?

Do they need a restaurant like yours?

If not, have you thought about opening a different kind of restaurant or going to another neighborhood?

GETTING STARTED

Your building

Have you found a good building for your restaurant?

Will you have enough room when your business gets bigger?

Can you fix the building the way you want it without spending too much money?

Can people get to it easily from parking spaces, bus stops, or their homes?

Have you had a lawyer check the lease and zoning?

Equipment and supplies

Do you know what equipment and supplies you need and how much they will cost?

Can you save some money by buying secondhand equipment?

Your merchandise

Have you decided what things you will sell?

Do you know how much or how many of each you will buy to open your restaurant with?

Have you found suppliers who will sell you what you need at a good price?

Have you compared the prices and credit terms of different suppliers?

Your records

Have you planned a system of records that will keep track of your income and expenses, what you owe other people, and what other people owe you?

Have you worked out a way to keep track of your inventory so that you will always have enough on hand for your customers but not more than you can sell?

Have you figured out how to keep your payroll records and take care of tax reports and payments?

Do you know what financial statements you should prepare?

Do you know how to use those financial statements?

Do you know an accountant who will help you with your records and financial statements?

Your restaurant and the law

Do you know what licenses and permits you need?

Do you know what business laws you have to obey?

Do you know a lawyer you can go to for advice and for help with legal papers?

Protecting your restaurant

Have you made plans for protecting your restaurant against thefts of all kinds—shoplifting, robbery, burglary, employee stealing?

Have you talked with an insurance agent about what kinds of insurance you need?

Buying a business someone else has started

Have you made a list of what you like and don't like about buying a business someone else has started?

Are you sure you know the real reason the owner wants to sell his business?

Have you compared the cost of buying the business with the cost of starting a new business?

Is the stock up to date and in good condition?

Is the building in good condition?

Will the owner of the building transfer the lease to you?

Have you talked with other businessmen in the area to see what they think of the business?

Have you talked with the suppliers?

Have you talked with a lawyer about it?

MAKING IT GO

Advertising

Have you decided how you will advertise? (Newspapers, posters, handbills, radio, by mail?)

Do you know where to get help with your ads?

Have you watched what other stores do to get people to buy?

The prices you charge

Do you know how to figure what you should charge for each item you sell?

Do you know what other restaurants like yours charge?

Buying

Do you have a plan for finding out what your customers want?

Will your plan for keeping track of your inventory tell you when it is time to order more and how much to order?

Do you plan to buy most of your stock from a few suppliers rather than a little from many, so that those you buy from will want to help you succeed?

Selling

Have you decided whether you will serve or use self-service?

Do you know how to get customers to buy?

Have you thought about why you like to buy from some salesmen while others turn you off?

Your employees

If you need someone to help you, do you know where to look?

Do you know what kind of person you need?

Do you know how much to pay?

Do you have a plan for training your employees?

A FEW EXTRA QUESTIONS

Have you figured out whether you could make more money working for someone else?

Does your family go along with your plan to start a business of your own?

Do you know where to find out about new ideas and new products?

Do you have a work plan for yourself and your employees?

Have you gone to the nearest Small Business Administration office for some help with your plans?

If your answer to all the questions is yes, you're in excellent shape. More than likely, though, you used the negative plenty of times. But all that means is that you have some more work to do before you're 100 percent ready. That's what this book is for—to help with the questions.

Do you still think running a small restaurant is for you? If so, read on. The restaurant business is a tough one, as is confirmed by the huge number of failures. You've heard the old saying that new restaurants are always needed because people have to eat. True, but there is nothing in the saying that says they've got to eat in your place. Running a small restaurant can be a rewarding experience if you know what you are doing. The purpose of this book is to give you an edge, because no matter how hard you're willing to work, you're going to need all the edge you can get to make your restaurant a going concern.

TWO

The Menu
and What It Means
to You

*What to Include / Balancing the Menu / Pricing for Profit /
Creating the Printed Menu*

LOOK AT THAT FOLDED PIECE OF CARDBOARD YOU PLOP DOWN in front of every customer. Is it frayed? Stained? Badly printed? Crammed full of runny mimeograph sheets? If it is, you are guilty of menu malice.

A menu is probably the single most important item in your restaurant. It performs three valuable functions. First, it is your own guide. It tells you what to purchase and when. Your entire business is based upon the descriptions in that piece of cardboard. The menu is a restaurant's soul, it defines your needs. Second, the menu provides a link between you and your customers. It tells them what you have to offer. And for your sake, it should sell the customer. A good menu can be a tremendous selling device if it offers stimulating descriptions and appetizing pictures of meals. And third, the menu provides a price range for your customers—the end result of your business, money.

So, planning a menu should not be carelessly tossed off the top of your head. It ties together your entire operation. A menu should be planned with great care.

WHAT TO INCLUDE

First, what should be on the menu? You must offer your customers what they want. Don't indulge yourself. Don't load the menu with poor-selling, exotic dishes. Escargots are fine if your restaurant's theme is French, but if you run a truck stop and snails are on the menu, you're headed for trouble. So know your customers. Discover what they like. Keep close tabs on the number and types of dinners you have sold over the past weeks and months. You may discover that you sold 120 fish-and-chips dinners one week, but only three stuffed-green-pepper dinners. After tallying up the numbers, you should have an idea about which to push and which to drop. But never be too hasty; be certain to check and recheck. For example, did the fish and chips sell better than the stuffed peppers because of the hot, summer weather, when lighter dishes are more popular? Research may indicate that stuffed peppers should be served during the autumn and winter months and dropped during the summer and spring.

A menu can be treated like a piece of clay. In the hands of a skilled restaurateur it can be shaped into many things. A menu never should be a static, unchanging, day-in-day-out dull list. Take advantage of seasons, holidays. Give your customers what they want, and make sure they want what you offer.

Is all this fuss about menus really necessary? Sandy's menu never changed. Even the gravy spots had been there for years. But since Sandy ran a small diner, it didn't seem to matter very much. She had steady customers and served good food at reasonable prices. You know scores of small restaurants like this. Some seem to go on forever; others aren't so lucky.

But what would have happened if Sandy had taken the time to plan a first-class menu? The total food costs would have plummeted. With a proper menu, Sandy would have been more in touch with customer wants. She could have dropped half the items on her ancient menu. The days when extensive menus meant quality are over. She would do more seasonal buying. Her food cost would be lower, and the fresh foods would raise the quality of her dishes. And a new menu would probably attract more customers—both new patrons and regulars coming back more often. An ever-changing and improving menu surprises and sells.

BALANCING THE MENU

What should the menu offer? A good deal depends on the restaurant's theme. Is it Chinese, Polynesian, Italian, general? In many cases the more "exotic" restaurants feel obliged to carry a small number of American-style foods, such as steak or chicken. But American tastes are becoming more sophisticated. Years ago all U.S. Chinese restaurants were Cantonese and served the bland food popular in Canton. Now operators are offering almost every type of Chinese regional cooking, including the regal Mandarin and the sometimes spicy Szechuan.

But no matter what type of restaurant you run—even if it is a more exotic one—you must offer a good, balanced menu. It should be nutritious and varied. Texture, flavor, color should all be considered, and foods should complement each other. The plate of food you put in front of your customer should present a pleasing sight, a mix of tantalizing aromas, and a variety of tastes. Food arrangement is an art in itself. A garnish of vivid green parsley and lemon wedges enhances a platter of golden-brown fish or fried clams. Cherry tomatoes add color and texture to uniform crisp green lettuce.

The menus should provide enough variety of choices to keep customers coming back. Even steak houses have two or three non-beef items like broiled chicken or fried butterfly shrimp. It pays to have light meals available for dieters and those with petite appetites. You'll discover that a menu with different foods is more interesting. A choice between shish kabob and codfish cakes is more desirable than a choice between pot roast and London broil. And don't forget the side dishes. A choice of green beans, corn, or lima beans for each and every dish is monotonous. Many restaurants fall down when it comes to the quality of the side dishes. They have a big pot of beans or corn and dish out lifeless, drained vegetables for each dinner. Even though they aren't the main part of the meal, they are important. The steak may be perfect, but a soggy, tasteless ear of corn can ruin the dinner. Take care at all levels. Make sure the tomato juice is cold and the coffee is hot.

PRICING FOR PROFIT

So much for the customer, now how about the owner? Your menu must provide you with a profit while reflecting a competitive pricing system. What it boils down to is, How much should you charge? There are a number of systems—some restaurant owners just double or treble the cost of the purchased food. But the best system is the one that takes every expense into account. That roast-pork dinner with mashed potatoes, applesauce, and asparagus has a lot of different expenses built into it. First and most obvious is the food cost. Each item in the raw form breaks down in cost to a specific amount of money. Add to that the labor cost. You or your chef prepared the food —you trimmed the pork and roasted it, you opened the applesauce, boiled the asparagus, arranged the plate. Some recipes cost more in labor and some cost more in basic food cost. Determine the price of the meal by considering all these facts. A breakdown of a dinner might look like this:

Fried-Clam Dinner, Breakdown

	Raw food cost
Fried clams	$ .50
Coleslaw	.10
French fries	.15
Total food cost	$ .75

Preparation time by chef: 5 minutes
Chef receives $5 per hour. 5 minutes = $\frac{1}{12}$ an hour

Labor cost = $.42

Total meal cost   (not including waiter's time
and general expenses) $1.17

A breakdown chart is a rough approximation, but it adds on major labor expenses, which are taking a growing bite out of restaurant profits.

Before you decide on a final price, look at what your competitors charge for similar meals. Don't price blind. If your prices are too high or your menu is dull, you will lose customers. On the other hand, if you charge too little, you may end up where you began—out of business.

Try to have a price mix as well as an entree mix. Both high-priced meals and budget meals have their place on your menu. If everything is high-cost, you'll scare away customers. If everything is low-cost, you are leaving out some popular items that many people want and can afford.

The pros and cons of the number of menu items can be defended from either side. But if you are a beginner, it only makes sense to sell a limited number of items. And even though you start small, and your menu may remain small, you should expand the number of offerings as the menu changes from week to week. Experimentation is a good way to help a business, even for an experienced owner. What works, keep. What fails, dump or save and try at a more opportune time.

In making a reasonable profit consider:

- Food costs.
- Labor costs.
- Your competitor's prices.
- Uniform portion control (don't serve six ounces of meat one time and twelve the next.)

It is difficult to keep in touch with everything; for instance, a cook may ruin a roast and dump it without telling you. But keep on top of everything as much as you can. You have a big advantage over a giant restaurant-chain manager with dozens of people and locations to worry about. You are right in the middle of the action. It's a matter of getting the knack of balancing all the elements in your head—to remember that you sold one hundred roast-pork dinners last week and that you got an average of twenty-one servings per roast. It is a challenge to know where every dime goes, but if you do know, the chances are that your operation will be a profitable one.

CREATING THE PRINTED MENU

Good menus are fantastic selling devices. Use them to your advantage. Menus come in all sizes, shapes, and expenses. Some are mimeographed sheets while others are large glossy works of art. A few restaurants don't even have menus—they just write out the day's list on a blackboard. But a menu is too good a device to waste. It is the very first thing your customer studies when he enters your restaurant. Put yourself in your customer's place. It is dinnertime, say six o'clock. You're hungry but not famished. You're considering just a hamburger. Then the waiter brings a menu. There is an eye-catching design on the front, maybe a clever welcome to the customer. Inside, the type is easy to read. The make-up of the copy pleases your eye. Interested, you read the descriptions of each dish. There's broiled Pompano: flown fresh from Florida. Snow-white flakes, drenched in a superb butter sauce with a hint of garlic. Sirloin steak: served on a sizzling hot platter. Charred on the outside and pink on the inside. Crisp fried onion rings and a gigantic baked Idaho topped with cool sour cream and chives.

The descriptions sell you. Suddenly you are hungrier than you thought you were. A hamburger just won't do. You've got to have that steak or fish. The delicious aromas wafting out from the kitchen also give the restaurant a big edge.

But don't stop with the main course. Consider the psychological state of the customer. Make sure that the menu returns for dessert, which should also be described as graphically as an X-rated movie. Tantalize each customer with words. Together with good service it sells a lot of food.

What is the best way to construct your menu? Some owners use the services of a professional consultant. A consultant can suggest a workable sequence and design the menu emphasizing your establishment's theme. But if you want to do your own menu, try to keep these pointers in mind:

- Make your menu easy to read. Have the printer use a large enough type face.
- Make it clear. If an entree is a la carte, make certain the customer can figure it out before he orders.

- Make your menu exciting. Give it a flavor all its own. Try to catch a few customers with it.
- Sell each item, but don't give all the same emphasis. Put steak ahead of the hamburger platter.
- Don't list according to price. Mix up the entries so your patrons don't order from the price list.
- Clip-ons should be strategically placed so they don't obscure important parts of the menu. How many times have you had to virtually rip a menu apart to discover all the offerings?
- Don't forget about breakfast and luncheon menus. They deserve as much care as the dinner menu. After all, the same principles work, no matter what the hour is.

Once a restaurant owner has sunk his hard-earned cash into a menu, it is often difficult to convince him or her that change is necessary. Don't let the expense of the menu dictate its use. It is better that you use a plain, well-written menu that you feel comfortable changing than a big, beautiful one that you consider too expensive to replace often.

Some restaurants use a variety of preplanned menus that are rotated by week or month. These menus mix up the types of offerings and take advantage of seasonal buys. But even this system should be experimented with. Don't get into the rut of using the same recipes over and over again.

Take a second look at your own menu. Does it do everything you want it to? Does it work well for you? If not, change it. If it does, change it anyway. Experiment. Try to come up with a more perfect formula. See if you can please your customers better while reflecting a more efficient operation in the kitchen. The menu—it's where your business is at.

THREE

Supplying Your Restaurant

How to Order / Receiving / Storage / Issuing

A RESTAURANT'S LIFE BLOOD IS ITS SUPPLIES. STOP THE flow of supplies, and the restaurant dies. As long as you pay your bills, it is improbable that the food supplies will be completely cut off. But between the time the raw foods leave the warehouse and the time you serve them to your patrons, there are dozens of ways profits can be siphoned off.

This chapter deals with the heart of your operation—the food. The first step is purchasing your supplies. In large operations the job is assigned to a steward. Unfortunately, small restaurants can't afford stewards, so this important task usually falls to the owner. Although you may be tempted to delegate the job to another employee, it makes sense for you to handle it. Why? Money. You'll find that few employees will be as interested as you are in saving money. Another reason to handle the buying personally is that a dishonest employee can steal you blind and wreck your business. He or she could buy from a more expensive purveyor in return for kickbacks or could even overorder and resell the extra. It has all happened. Even if the employee is honest, he or she may feel like taking the easy way out by ordering from a convenient but expensive purveyor, something no owner with a healthy regard for profit would do.

Purchasing requires a solid background in the subject. There are many things to learn—food grades, how to order, quantities, market fluctuations, and prices. In some ways it is easier for the owner to handle purchasing, because he has his finger in all the restaurant's pies. He knows what sold last week, where the waste was, when the menu is changed. His big problem is organization.

HOW TO ORDER

There are a number of ways to order supplies, but the most common for small-restaurant owners is open market buying. This method is simply predetermining the need for a day or a week, then contacting three or four different purveyors to fix the lowest prices with the highest quality. Long-term contracts are profitable for items needed on a daily basis, like bread and milk.

There is much to remember when ordering. It is all too easy to get swept off your feet when you are offered what looks like a tremendous buy. But buying for a restaurant is different from buying for an individual family. A restaurant buys in quantity and quality. Yield is all-important. A pound of fatty chuck may initially cost less than a leaner pound, but after the fat melts away in the cooking, the leaner chuck may give a better price per pound. While one pound makes little difference to an individual family, multiply one pound by one hundred and you'll see how important it is to a small restaurant.

It's important also that you pay by weight instead of by any other form of measurement. Sides of beef or cases of eggs can vary dramatically in actual poundage.

In purchasing meat, poultry, and fish, take the fat, bones, and waste into account. Fillets or pretrimmed, boned meat can be a better buy than the unprocessed items.

How much should you buy? The only answer is to look at the menu for the next week: how much do you expect to sell, based on how much you have sold over the past few weeks? You make the best educated guess possible. No one knows the future, and sometimes your forecasts will be wrong. During the 1976 Democratic Convention in New York City several restaurants near Madison Square Garden anticipated tremendous increases in volume. They took on more help and ordered more supplies. Unfortunately, they guessed wrong. A number of circumstances, such as the delegates eating in other parts of the city and police barricades, actually decreased business from the week before. Another difficult time to predict is after an advertising campaign. If the campaign is successful, business may increase 50 percent. If unsuccessful, it may not increase at all. Results: oversupplied restaurants. As owner, though, you should be in pretty good touch with the number of customers expected. All forecasting can do is predict the future based on the past. If you have a good idea about how past events affected business, the future shouldn't present too much trouble.

How should you purchase? It is vital that you know exactly what you want before you get on the phone. Don't order supplies haphazardly. If the supplier delivers two or three times a day, the cost is yours. Be certain the purveyor has your exact order, the amount, the quantity, and the quality. The vendor must be provided with clear, precise instructions. He must know what standards you expect. Keep a copy of the transactions for receiving the food, since you will have to check everything to be sure all is in order.

Unless you run a vegetarian restaurant, you'll find that meat will take a huge chunk of your expenses. Learn all the grades and cuts. You may find that you don't need the highest grade or a special cut or you'll need a mixture of grades.

If you use a large amount of canned foods, you should run can-cutting tests. Get samples from different vendors and check the contents for quality, weight—label, actual, and drained— and number of portions. You'll then be able to identify the supplier that provides the highest quality at the best price.

It makes sense to maintain a good relationship with your purveyors. Always pay your bills promptly and be completely fair. Good, steady customers who can be trusted deserve and get better service then the others during food crunches. So keep your relationship with the salespeople on a solid business footing. You may discover that your "good friend" who has "taken care" of you for years actually has been sticking you with a higher price tag than other vendors who aren't so friendly. You run a business in which food costs are the major expense. Laxity in purchasing destroys profits—keep it up and you'll really see red.

RECEIVING

After you have purchased the food, try to arrange for a convenient delivery time. A truckload of frozen foods delivered during the lunch rush hour is bad planning. It is vital that you oversee every single item before you sign for the shipment. You have to check quality and quantity on order forms and specification sheets. Check off each item as it fits the bill. You need a set of scales to weigh different meats and produce. If something doesn't meet your specifications, this is the proper time to yell. Don't accept it.

Most purveyors are honest, but there are always a few who aren't. Therefore you'll be looking for mistakes. Keep your eye out for lower grades, short weights, and wrong items. No matter how rushed you are, it is good policy never to let anything be taken straight from the delivery truck to the storage room, freezers, or refrigerators. Demand what you paid for, no matter how annoyed the salesman may be or how inconvenient it might be for him at that moment.

After accepting the food, date everything, since it is good policy to use supplies in the order they were received. The shipment of the twenty-eighth should be used after the shipment of the twenty-first.

STORAGE

You've purchased your supplies carefully, getting the best buy. And you have carefully checked every single item received, turning back anything that didn't meet your specifications. But you aren't out of the woods yet. There are plenty of pitfalls that can mushroom your costs and destroy your profits.

Storage is vital. After receiving a shipment, you must store all items in their proper places, especially perishables and frozen foods.

There are three types of storage areas: the dry storeroom, the freezer, and the refrigerator. There are three basic rules to storage:

- The area must be easily cleaned and kept sanitary.
- The proper temperature must be set.
- An orderly system of storage must be utilized.

In a dry storeroom you must fight against infestations of vermin. Unless you are diligent, rats and all types of insects will turn your larder into a picnic site. Be especially careful with cereals, grains, and flour. Insect larvae thrive in and on them. And a clean refrigerator is mandatory. If one item goes bad, the odor can affect the taste of milk, cream, butter, and other delicate foods.

Everyone knows that temperature is important in freezers and refrigerators, but different temperature and humidity levels can harm your food.

Meats should be kept at a temperature between 32 and 36 degrees Fahrenheit. Fruits and vegetables need to be stored at 35 to 45 degrees. Dairy products keep best at temperatures between 38 and 46 degrees. Both meats and dairy products do best when the relative humidity is between 75 and 85 percent, while fruits and vegetables thrive in a range of 85 to 95 percent relative humidity.

Even a dry storeroom is not immune to changing temperature levels. Too much heat in the dry storeroom can affect even canned and processed foods, which deteriorate at high temperatures. And the warmer it gets, the more the insects, mold, and bacteria will flourish. The storeroom should be kept as dry as possible. A hot, damp storeroom will cause food spoilage. Ideally, the temperature of the storeroom should be around 50 to 55 degrees.

When you store food, do it systematically. Don't shove crates and boxes into spaces helter-skelter. A good owner will audit stocks constantly. A loose storage system invites abuses of food supplies by employees. Remember, efficiency doesn't matter to the employees. It only matters to you, the owner who pays the bills.

ISSUING

Even though your operation is small, don't make the mistake of letting everyone into the storage areas to take food as they wish. To keep tabs on where the food goes, you must keep records and have an orderly system. Think about it. After a shipment, it looks like the supplies are inexhaustible. The temptation to let nature take its course is great. Large restaurants put special employees in charge of the stockroom and have systems using requisition forms. A small restaurant can't afford a special employee just to take care of food, but you must keep track of the food used. Put yourself or a trusted employee in charge of the storage areas. Then keep the storage areas locked to everyone else. When stores are needed, you issue the food, keeping track of what is taken and by whom. It doesn't matter if you use a printed checklist or a notebook as long as you understand where every ounce of food is going.

Keeping the storerooms locked also prevents pilfering. Many restaurants, lax with their supplies, often lose supplies that go home in the back seat of their employees' cars. It's easy—a roast here, a few steaks there, a nice jar of mayonnaise, a couple of cans of tomato juice—who's going to know? And the sad thing is that many employees don't see this pilfering as stealing. They're getting even with the boss for a denied raise. Or the storage room is seen as communal property. The waitress didn't have time to shop that day, so she "borrows" a few items. Sooner or later you may find out who your pilferers are, but that's locking the barn door after the horse has gotten out. Make it difficult in the first place by locking the storage area up tight and keeping the key. Don't let that hidden cost appear in the first place.

To summarize, in purchasing, receiving, storage, and issuing, your objective is to keep in touch with every scrap of food from start to finish. Poor judgment or carelessness in any of these areas can close you down.

FOUR

Planning
for Best Results

Design and Layout / Equipment / Laws

DESIGN AND LAYOUT

Do YOUR WAITRESSES EVER COLLIDE WITH THE COOK? DO customers at the far end of the restaurant complain about slow service? Is your cook's station dirty? Maybe the problem isn't your employees, maybe the fault is in the design of your restaurant.

Improper design can cost you money through wasted time, unhappy employees, dissatisfied customers, and, in extreme cases, an unfriendly department of sanitation.

If you are just starting out, take time to think out every detail of your restaurant's design. If you are already in business and stuck with a poorly designed kitchen or storage area, there are solutions. Although the person starting out has a clean slate, the owner who is already in business knows from experience what areas need redesigning.

In the design and layout of your restaurant, the primary point to remember is that the entire operation should be geared to provide the customer with a meal quickly and efficiently. The process of getting food from the kitchen to the customer must be smooth and uncomplicated. Think of it as an assembly line: there is a continuous forward progression, starting with raw materials and ending up with the finished product. An assembly line that has to stop, reverse itself, and move sideways is obviously inefficient.

The same is true in the operation of a restaurant. If you have it arranged so that the salad is at the end of the assembly line while the hot food is first, you have a bad system. The result is the reverse of what makes sense: salad first and hot food last. If a waitress has to check the kitchen in person six or seven times for her orders, productivity is being wasted. The ideal situation is a direct and logical progression: the order is received, and the food is taken from the storage area, prepared, processed, picked up by the waitress, and served to the customer. That's what you have to shoot for.

With the idea of a smooth operation, how do you start planning? Take every single detail into account. Receiving, storage, food preparation, the cooking area, sanitation, dishwashing, service, dining area, rest rooms, and parking. Within each area you must decide the type of equipment and where it will go: will you put in booths, tables, or both, and what layout will best facilitate service?

Small-restaurant owners should pay attention to the details of planning their operations, the same as large-restaurant owners. Some owners think their restaurants aren't large enough to matter. But planning that saves time and labor translates itself into profits, sometimes the margin of operation that keeps the ship afloat.

For example, Sal ran a small café in a shopping center. He had both counter and table service. Sal, a chef-owner, did his own cooking and did it well. He employed two part-time waitresses and a dishwasher. His menu was all short-order, and his kitchen equipment was in full view of the customers. Sal's big problem was that he didn't have a well-designed system. His freezer was stuck in a back room, his grill was at the wrong end of the counter, and the refrigerator was a good twenty steps at the other end. The coffeemaker and hot-water dispenser were smack in the middle. This layout was fine as long as there weren't too many customers around. In order to serve a simple hamburger, Sal had to trudge to the refrigerator for the pattie, go to the opposite end and slap it on the grill, race to the cutting area, which was next to the coffeemaker, to prepare the bun and trimmings. While this was going on, his employees would be scurrying up and down behind the counter, setting places, pouring water, making coffee, and picking up table orders—running into each other. Sal and his waitresses crossed each other's paths a thousand times during the day. When the lunch crush came, the orders stacked up like Christmas planes to Miami. In addition, the waitress couldn't get the dirty dishes back to the dishwasher and wait on tables at the same time, so the dishes were stacked up in a corner until the dishwasher picked them up himself. Needless to say, the customers weren't happy with the slow service and confusion. Sal finally went out of business in order to do something less nerve-racking— wrestling alligators.

There was a solution to Sal's problem: redesign. He should have brought everything he needed—refrigerator, grill, work station—together. The other employees still would be moving behind him, but Sal would have been stationary. He, the head of the operation, wouldn't have been rushing around wasting time, energy, and money. The orders could have been finished quickly, keeping the customers happy.

EQUIPMENT

Equipment can also cause planning problems. Marty, another small-restaurant entrepreneur, got a good deal on the highest-quality, up-to-date broilers, slicers, blenders, mixers, and other kitchen equipment. But three months later he discovered that most of the food he used was prepackaged. He wasn't getting much use out of his fancy gadgets. The end result was a big money loss. Make sure that you buy only what you use. Don't go overboard when you see a new electric crepemaker if your hottest seller is hamburgers.

LAWS

Basically, in planning you must keep three separate factors in mind: the government, the restaurant personnel, and the customer. Have you arranged everything within the law? There are fire, safety, labor, and sanitation laws to be obeyed. Make sure you are aware of them.

You and your employees must be considered. There are

labor laws that mandate locker rooms, ventilation, and clean facilities, and your restaurant should be a convenient and pleasant place to work. The kitchen shouldn't be overcrowded, your operating systems should be efficient, and every employee from the chef to the dishwasher should be given sufficient working area. If you and your employees perform all tasks efficiently, productivity will soar. Never lose sight of your objective: to get the food out to the customer as quickly as possible.

The customer: the final link. He or she receives the end result of all your work. Plan the dining room so that it is uncongested. If a waitress has to march a mile from the kitchen to a customer in a corner, the quality of the food will drop along the way, so arrange your seating so there will be no out-of-the-way corners. The dining area—all of it—should be snuggled up tightly against the kitchen.

It may seem obvious that the ultimate goal of planning is to serve the customer effectively and quickly, but many restaurants lose sight of the goal. Think about it this way: the faster a customer is served, the sooner he eats and the happier he will be. And the sooner he finishes his meal, the sooner another customer can take his place and begin the process anew. Higher efficiency means higher turnover. Higher turnover means more profits. And happy customers mean both.

FIVE

Advertising and Promoting Your Restaurant

Meeting the Competition / Market Research / Restaurant Identity / Advertising / Publicity / Continuing the Sell

IT IS 3:15 P.M. THERE'S NOT A SOUL IN YOUR RESTAURANT. All your employees are puttering around like retarded rabbits, preparing for the dinner crowd. Suddenly it hits you: what a dreadful waste of labor and time! There should be customers in here now. The question is, How?

Or, it is 6 P.M. on a Wednesday. It's your busiest time of day, but less than half the normal number of patrons are sitting in your dining room. And you've been noticing every Wednesday that fewer and fewer customers come in. Then you discover that a seafood restaurant competitor three blocks away has a special fish-and-clam fry every Wednesday. How do you get your customers back?

Maybe business is just bad and getting worse, you reason dejectedly. You can't understand it. Your food is good and your service is terrific, but business has been going downhill since that restaurant across the street began featuring a salad bar and an all-you-can-eat smorgasbord. How can you get your customers back?

How to recapture old customers and draw in new ones? That is the eternal question. It's the name of the game in big restaurants. Restaurants cannot exist without customers.

MEETING THE COMPETITION

The customer is the objective, but unfortunately your restaurant is not alone in its search for the quarry. There are hundreds of different eating establishments trying to lure customers out of your place and into theirs. This is called competition. If you're not bothered with competition, you've apparently been issued the first franchise on Mars. There are different levels, however, of competition. A seafood restaurant doesn't present the kind of competition to a Mandarin Chinese restaurant that another Mandarin Chinese restaurant would. But in the broad sense, all restaurants are competing for money-paying customers. If you can't handle the competition, you probably will join the swelling ranks of former restaurant owners.

In any competition you need an edge, a reason for the customer to select you. You need to convince customers that your restaurant is exactly what they want.

There are three things to keep in mind:

(1) Find out who your customers are and what they like.
(2) Make your establishment well known to as many people as possible.
(3) Keep your restaurant's standards high, because you have only one shot at a new customer.

MARKET RESEARCH

Before you embark on your advertising campaign, do a little market research. All this means is that you need to know as much as possible about where your business comes from—where your customers live, what they like in general, what they like or dislike about your restaurant. How do you do this? One way is to be straightforward. Ask them. You can make up a questionnaire or interview them yourself. Of course, you also have a good deal of basic information in your guest checks. They tell you the average meal price and what menu item is most popular. This is an important point. For example, you may find that both your fried-shrimp platter and your one-pound lobster are real crowd pleasers. If so, it may be worth your while to set aside slower days and use these dinners as specials to draw in more business.

After you've learned as much as possible, get back to your competition. It always pays to know what the other guy is doing, especially if he is taking business away from you. If the competition is doing something that works, study it. Never, however, copy a competitor's idea. Just get a better idea that he will have to copy. Always take the offensive. Do what is right for your restaurant and you'll be the pace setter.

RESTAURANT IDENTITY

Which brings us to establishing your restaurant's own identity. This is one of the most important steps in promoting your restaurant. You have got to have something different, something that makes your restaurant stand apart from the crowd. Suppose you own a steak house that fronts on a highway, and there are five or six other steak houses within three miles of yours, all competing for the same customers. How do you get the customers to stop at your place rather than one of the others?

First, separate yourself from the pack. Get a theme. Instead of the usual ho-hum display sign that proclaims: "Steaks and Chops, Made the Way You Like 'Em," be descriptive: "Thick, sizzling sirloins, done Maverick's way." Instead of naming your restaurant "The Steak House," try something that would stick in the customer's mind. Be different. Be creative. You must make people sit up and take notice.

Once you have a good theme, get a decor to match. Wagon wheels and antique tools à la the old West are good today. But go further. For instance, you may make up a special brand for your restaurant or put a salad bar into an old buckboard with the establishment's logo burnt into the side. There are any number of gimmicks to try. If they work, keep them. If they don't, think up something else. For example, you may want to have a special corral night when you give away miniature brands or inexpensive giveaways, such as glasses, napkins, postcards, or swizzle sticks with your logo plastered all over them. Keep your name in circulation. Don't be afraid to be different.

You've thought up a special theme and you are proud of everything about your restaurant. The next step is to get its name into the minds of thousands of potential customers. Your restaurant is like the movie stars you see on TV talk shows. The movie star is on the talk show to get exposure, to plug his latest movie. The more attention the star receives, the more successful the movie will be and the more money the star can command for the next movie.

You are looking for exactly the same kind of exposure for your restaurant. You want people to think of you every time they get hungry. Advertising, publicity, public relations, direct mail, word of mouth—all can get you exposure and customers when utilized properly.

ADVERTISING

Everyone knows what advertising is. We are surrounded by ads for everything imaginable. Ads are used on radio, TV, magazines, newspapers, journals. Ads are sometimes mailed directly to the customer. With so many different ways to reach people, you must consider which is the best for your situation. As a small-restaurant owner, you can't afford a large-scale Madison Avenue TV blitz. Small restaurants are usually forced to do the advertising work themselves. Try it. But you'll discover it is not as easy as it looks.

You can't blindly hand some copy to a newspaper and think that you are doing effective advertising. Your ad has to have a hook that will attract the reader or listener's attention. It should reach the potential customer personally. An effective ad talks: "Maverick's: where you play for high steaks." And last, the ad must be clear and concise. Don't belabor a point. Use the fewest number of words and make absolutely sure the ad is clear enough to be understood by everyone over the age of six.

How much advertising should you do? This is where your market research helps. If most of your customers live within two or three miles of you, it doesn't pay to advertise in a paper whose readership is ten miles away—unless, of course, you think can draw customers from that distance for one reason or another. Don't go overboard. While it is best to reach as many people as possible, it is clearly unprofitable to risk your advertising dollars on people who live too far away.

Don't forget publications other than newspapers. Take a careful look at your local newsstand. Perhaps there is a theater magazine that would be an ideal medium for promoting your restaurant. Local, inexpensive radio stations can be good. Television tends to be too expensive for most small restaurants, unless you want to advertise at four in the morning, which is not recommended.

Look around you. Go to the library and see what local papers, magazines, and bulletins are available. The phone book is a must. Many people turn to the yellow pages when trying to decide where to go. An ad that describes your restaurant in the best light will go much further in convincing a potential patron than just a name and a phone number. And if you do use an agency, never forget who is boss. Don't be afraid to change your ad if it isn't doing the job. And don't let a rushed copywriter snow you—you have to try to get the best. You might look into the possibility of trying an agency for a limited time only.

PUBLICITY

Advertising is not the only way to get your restaurant's name in print. The smart owner will capitalize on publicity and public relations. Publicity for the establishment never hurts (as long as it is good—publicity like: "Smokey Dog Cage Poisons 45 with Spoiled Tuna Fish" is definitely out). There are many ways to keep your business in the public eye. Sponsor a little-league team, a bowling team. Have an annual "Athlete of the Year" dinner party at which you honor the top sports hero from the local high school. Make sure that the local press knows in advance about the celebration, and the paper will provide you with free advertising. You might even send a photograph along with your press release to attract more attention and to increase the likelihood that your story will be used.

If something happens in your restaurant—either arranged by you or by luck—write a press release and send it to local papers and radio and television stations. If your chef invents a new dish to commemorate the landing on Mars or the invention of the telephone, there may be an interesting story for a news-hungry editor.

It helps to have a good relationship with the press. Publicity, however, is a two-edged sword: sometimes what the editor wants is what you want to keep out of the paper. Be careful to get all your facts straight when you send in a press release. Once stung with wrong facts, the paper is very likely to ignore you.

CONTINUING THE SELL

Now that you have made your name through advertising and publicity, what do you do next? If you have planned your restaurant well, you don't have to do anything at all. In fact, if you haven't been preparing for new customers, your time and money have been squandered. Advertising and publicity give potential customers just a taste to get them past your front door. Once the customer is inside, the *coup de grâce* is delivered by the positive aspects of your restaurant. The ads and gimmicks must be backed up by good, solid food and excellent service, and a pleasing atmosphere.

It can get tricky if the ads bring in an overflow of new customers. Jerry, owner of the Sea Saloon, made a very bad mistake when he advertised a fried-clam special at half price. He didn't foresee the extra five hundred customers. The result was that his employees were swamped with work, the customers had to wait as long as an hour for service, and toward the end of the evening he ran out of clams. You have to look ahead and figure out the consequences of your actions. If you normally handle 100 dinners a night, with only five disgruntled customers, you are much better off than if you were to serve 300 dinners that pleased only 50 people, leaving 250 people to bad-mouth you all over town.

When the customer enters your restaurant, the sell must continue. You have a lot of advantages. Normally the customer is hungry, and the delightful aromas drifting out from the kitchen make him or her very receptive to further selling. The menu should describe the foods in mouth-watering detail, preferably with appetizing photographs, and if possible, you should arrange for a food display.

SIX

The Importance of Good Sanitation

Illnesses Caused by Poor Sanitation / Planning Your Layout with Sanitation in Mind

HOW MANY TIMES HAVE YOU HEARD PEOPLE SAY, "IF YOU knew what goes on in restaurant kitchens, you'd never eat or drink anything they serve—not even a glass of water"? Many people do not think highly of restaurant sanitation, and in some instances they are correct. But sanitation departments have been busy cracking down on violators, and newspapers have resorted to publishing lists of the offending "dirty" establishments. For example, the *New York Times* publishes regularly the names and addresses of restaurants that have violated that city's Health Code—and some customers will never return to a place after it has been cited, even if the violation is corrected.

Customers just do not understand what a big job it is to keep any eating establishment clean. Unfortunately, quite a few restaurant operators don't appear to understand either. And that is a grave problem. Good sanitation practices are more than important—they are vital. Sanitation goes hand in hand with food preparation, storage, and serving; it should never be out of the mind of any owner or his employees.

You can't turn around in a restaurant without stumbling over something that affects the establishment's sanitation problems. For example, sanitation includes employees: How clean are they? Do they carry any contagious germs? Are they careless with food? It includes the food: Has it been prepared correctly? Have the proper precautions been taken with the perishable items, such as the milk, seafood, and poultry? Are the refrigerators and freezers set at the proper temperatures? Are the storage and work areas free of vermin? Consider the kitchen: Is the equipment easily cleanable? Do the employees keep it sanitary? Is the dishwater hot enough? And is the garbage disposed of properly? Are the restrooms clean and well-supplied with towels?

Now maybe you understand why sanitation is one of the small-restaurant owner's biggest headaches. But there are remedies for the problem. The first step is to understand all the laws regarding sanitation that affect you. It can cost you money, time, and customers if you disobey the law. Never forget that the government has the power to shut your operation down, or to give you sufficient bad publicity to shut you down through lack of business. Get yourself a copy of your local Health Department Code, and study the sections that apply to food establishments.

After you know what is expected of you, get organized. Organize everything and everyone. You must make sure that every single employee is involved. Make sure that they understand that a major part of their job is to keep the restaurant sanitary. Employees working with food must be cautioned against working while they are sick, and the owners must be certain that everyone obeys personal hygiene standards.

Employees also should understand that they are expected to keep their stations clean at all times. It saves time and effort if you have your employees clean several times during the course of the day. It is a mistake to pick a single time at the end of the day to clean. First, you have a big, tough job instead of many littles ones. Second, at the end of a hard, long day no one really feels like mopping and scrubbing, so chances are that you'll have the same problem staring you in the face next morning—after a night of hardening and germ breeding.

Since you want your employees to devote some of their time to cleaning and you want them to do it well, incorporate any cleaning jobs into the training program for any new employees. And make sure that you stress the importance of cleaning—it is as important as any other job. How many times have you seen a waitress take a few careless swipes at a table top with a rag black with grease? Have you caught a dishwasher just rinsing off a spoon or a plate with cold water because it didn't look too dirty? And then there is the chef who thinks nothing of coming to work with a case of the flu.

There are important reasons to be strict when it comes to sanitation. In one word, *germs*. Whether you like it or not, we live in a dirty, germ-filled world. So what if that shipment of frozen foods thawed out and was refrozen? Did it really matter that the can of green beans was rusty and bulging at the top? The heavy cream for the strawberries was left out under the hot lights for four hours—is there really a problem?

The answer to why you should be extremely careful should be obvious. Not only would the effect on business be far from good if half of your patrons suddenly came down with food poisoning, but you would certainly be stuck with many messy lawsuits as well. It is in the restaurant owner's interest to serve the customer well—and safely.

ILLNESSES CAUSED BY POOR SANITATION

There are a variety of illnesses that can be transmitted through improperly prepared or carelessly handled food. Probably the most common illness associated with food poisoning is caused by staphylococcus micro-organisms. These tiny creatures flourish in warmer temperatures. They start growing slowly at room temperature (68 degrees) and more rapidly as the temperature rises. There is no protection against these germs—they are everywhere. That is why temperature is so important. At a temperature of 82 to 86 degrees, it takes only five hours for enough poison to be produced to cause illness. And the illness appears relatively suddenly (one to five hours), so even if your customers don't get sick right in your restaurant, they certainly will know where they got it. And if you have ever had the awful experience of suffering through two or three days of violent sickness, you'll understand why the customer may think twice about returning to the scene of the crime.

There are many other illnesses that can be transmitted through restaurant food—salmonella food infection, botulism, and trichinosis to name three. Salmonella germs can be spread through improperly prepared food or infected humans. Its symptoms are similar to staphylococcus. Botulism is a rare disease most commony associated with improper canning or infected shellfish. This disease is deadly—over half of its victims die. Trichinosis is caused by microscopic worms that can infest pork. The only way to be safe is to cook pork products extremely well. Also, don't use the same grinder for beef and pork. A rare hamburger can carry trichinosis if there is a tiny bit of infested pork mixed in.

You won't get any compliments for keeping your customers healthy. But that certainly sounds wonderful if you've ever experienced the alternative.

PLANNING YOUR LAYOUT WITH SANITATION IN MIND

The layout of your establishment is also important for sanitation. It is essential that every nook and corner can be cleaned. This means having mobile equipment that can be pulled away from walls.

Good shelving is a blessing. Modern, pull-out shelves make cleaning chores much easier. The shelves can be swung out so there isn't a problem with moving food around.

Make sure that you have plenty of sinks that are in easy reach of your employees. It doesn't hurt to have a constant reminder out in the open. A lonely sink stuck off in a corner runs the risk of being forgotten.

Look into automatic equipment; it may be worth your while. For example, a power floor scrubber does a much better job more efficiently than a man with a mop. You also have to consider the reduced labor costs. A self-cleaning oven may cost much more initially, but when you compare it with the time involved in cleaning a standard oven over a number of years the self-cleaning oven becomes a good buy.

A major problem is garbage disposal. Do you have a huge, open bin of garbage out in vour parking lot, attracting cats, dogs, and flies—and repelling customers? Maybe you could use a compactor or, at least, a less unsightly way of getting rid of your waste.

Ultimately, your restaurant's sanitation depends on you, the owner or manager. You can organize and train your employees to do any job well, but never forget that the carelessness and slips can come back to haunt you. Try to be in the background, never losing touch with the sanitation operation. All it takes is that one container of cream left out for five little hours to make your life miserable and possibly destroy your business.

SEVEN

Successful Hiring
and Training Techniques

High Turnover and Other Employee Problems / How to
Look for Employees / Selecting the Best / Training

HIGH TURNOVER AND OTHER EMPLOYEE
PROBLEMS

F RANK'S GRILL LOST THREE EMPLOYEES DURING ONE THREE-
week stretch. One left quite suddenly; he gave no reason,
just picked up his last check and never came back. Two were
fired, one for taking days off without notice, and the other for
carting off steaks and roasts.

A high turnover like this is serious to a small establishment
like Frank's, where there are only four full-time employees. It
costs hard, cold cash each time a restaurant loses an employee.
The cost of breaking in a new employee has been estimated at
anywhere from $50 to $150. For an owner like Frank, whose
employees often stick to the job for a month or less, this adds
There are other serious problems besides the financial cost.
Unlike large restaurants, which can afford the time and expense
for complex training, the small restaurant must suffer along
with inexperienced help. One or two inexperienced people are
not a major headache if there are fifty others who are experienced. But in a small establishment with three or four employees, anyone untrained or inexperienced will stick out like
a sore thumb.

Many restaurant owners and managers don't seem to realize
the importance of the quality of their employees. A customer
is served by a waiter or waitress, eats food prepared by the

chef, and eats off plates washed by the dishwasher. The restaurant's reputation depends on the smoothness of service, the quality and appearance of the meal, and the cleanliness of the dishes. Your customers could care less that you are the best money manager in the business. To them, what your employees do for them is what counts.

Your employees can make or break you. And a surprising number of restaurants have failed because of high employee turnover. The person you hire is an extension of yourself. The waiter who snarls at the customers and then mixes up his orders is your representative to the great buying public.

HOW TO LOOK FOR EMPLOYEES

Okay, so employees are important. How do you find good ones? Frank hired many people by putting a torn, grease-spattered cardboard sign in the window. All it said was "Help Wanted," without even specifying the job available. Of course there are no sure-fire ways of hiring the perfect employee every time, but the first thing to do is get that sign out of the window and go through solid channels.

There are many ways to hunt for employees. First see if any friends or acquaintances you have in the restaurant business have any suggestions. If you have some employees who have worked out well, ask them to recommend friends. The people closest to you may have good ideas.

There are many organizations you can get in touch with. If you want to help society while looking for an employee, try getting in touch with foundations for the handicapped, rehabilitation centers, veterans' bureaus, and church groups. Local business clubs or organizations can offer good leads too.

It is possible you may want to work through an employment agency. In larger cities there are agencies that specialize in restaurant personnel. One caution: you have the last word, so get the person you want, not the one the agency wants to give you. Double-check references yourself. Also, make sure that you understand the fee arrangement. Sometimes the employer pays the fee, and sometimes the employee pays it. Public agencies are free.

And, of course, you can advertise for your employee in a local paper. Study the ads first to get an idea of what to list your job under and what to say. In your ad, make clear the type of job and the qualifications for it. There are two ways of handling newspaper responses. You can print your address or telephone number with the ad and have applicants drop by or phone for an interview, or you can have them mail you their qualifications in a letter or résumé. The advantage of the second method is that you can weed out the undesirable ones and set up interviews with the most promising responses.

SELECTING THE BEST

The next step is selecting your employee. Have everyone fill out an application form. This sheet of paper provides you with all your basic information about the individual applying for the job.

SAMPLE APPLICATION FORM

NAME· Last _____ First _____ Middle ____ Date ____

Address _____ Phone no. _____

Social Security no. _____

Date of birth _____ Height _____ Weight _____

Place of birth _____ No. of dependents _____

Single ___ Married ___ Divorced ___ Widowed ___ Separated ___

EDUCATION

Name and Address	From	To	Graduated
Elementary			
High School			
College			
Other			

Person to notify in case of accident _____

Address _____ Phone _____

Experience (List last employer first)	Dates	Job	Reason for leaving
Firm _____	From		
Address _____	To		
Supervisor _____			
Firm _____	From		
Address _____	To		
Supervisor _____			
Firm _____	From		
Address _____	To		
Supervisor _____			

U.S. Citizen ____ Health: Good ____ Fair ____ Poor ____

Minimum salary expected _____

List handicaps, chronic ailments, serious illnesses _____

This is merely minimum information. There may be many other areas in which you want more information.

Next, interview the applicants. There is no substitute for the personal touch. But there is a right and wrong way to approach an interview. Be friendly; you'll find out more if both of you are at ease with each other. Know beforehand what questions you want to ask. Be careful not to ask any questions that are irrelevant to the job—or even illegal. After you ask the question, listen to the answer very carefully. You'd be surprised at how many interviewers fall in love with their own voices and don't pay attention to how the questions are answered. And make sure you understand the applicant's response. If something isn't clear ask him or her to rephrase it for you. Above all, let the applicant ask you questions. You often find out more about a person by his or her questions than you do by any answer. Takes notes, making sure you jot something down that will enable you to remember the applicant later.

After you have interviewed several people, think over how they stack up against one another. Look at the notes you took during the interview. Think about how their personalities struck you. Was that second man what you had in mind for a waiter? It is obvious that if someone comes to an interview all rumpled and smelling like a locker room or a saloon, he or she is not the person you want to serve your customers.

Before hiring, check all the applicant's references. Don't be embarrassed to give the last employer listed a call. If the reference is in order, terrific, but if you discover it's a phony—well, it's better to catch the lie before you put the person in charge of your cash register.

By the way, don't throw away the application forms of the people you didn't like. Keep them well at hand. You never can tell when another opening may become available. And sometimes when the first selection doesn't work out, number two may come through.

TRAINING

"I quit, your dirty @#***!" Those words can strike terror into any small-restaurant owner's soul, especially during the rush hours. But it does happen fairly frequently in this business. Restaurant personnel have a higher rate of turnover than personnel in any other field.

A major reason is the lack of good training. Try taking someone right off the street and shoving them into the spot you need filled. It's like forcing a round peg into a square hole. If you are lucky—and sometimes you will be—after a clumsy week or two the new employee will settle into a routine. If you are not lucky you will find your establishment running through a great number of employees. You may need a revolving door.

A successful restaurant, big or small, is almost always an efficient business. A new employee reduces the efficiency of the business, because he or she can't immediately fit into the restaurant's operation, and causes a breakdown in the establishment's system.

What are some of the problems you face when hiring someone new? First, the new employee can be upset by the job's pressure. Next, your other employees may resent the new employee's inability to handle as much work as they do. Customers, of course, won't like the sloppy service they get during the breaking-in period. And you, the owner, won't be pleased with loss of money and efficiency. So for everyone concerned it is best that the new employee's transition period be as smooth as possible.

An example of how not to train a new employee took place at Frank's Grill. Frank hired Charlene as a waitress. She replaced the waiter who had been carting off steaks with his dirty uniforms. Charlene explained to Frank that she was a housewife returning to work. She had a little experience as a waitress, but that was ten years ago.

Frank patted Charlene on the shoulder and told her that she had nothing to worry about. He then explained her duties to her once and put her in charge of the ex-waiter's station. Frank then forgot all about Charlene. A week later she stormed into his office and quit. Once again Frank was in need of another employee.

Frank started out right when he explained the job's duties to Charlene. But it should not have stopped there. A new employee is not a separate unit that can be plugged in like a clock and expected to work perfectly. There is always a learning process. Frank made his big mistake by not looking at the whole picture. He saw Charlene only as someone he needed working at full capacity, and *now*. He neglected to take her feelings into account. Charlene had the potential to be an excellent employee; she was bright, eager, and willing to work. She just needed a little extra help to make it. By not handling her properly, Frank lost a potentially fine worker.

What should Frank have done? The very first thing would have been to lower his expectation of what a new employee could accomplish. In Charlene's case it was difficult because the other waitresses were clamoring for immediate help, but in the long run it is essential to be understanding. A new employee is thrust into a new environment that is strange and often terrifying. He or she can feel out of place and uneasy. It is up to the owner and the other employees to go out of their way and make anyone new feel accepted and a part of things.

Frank also should have told the other waitresses that he expected them to do the extra work until Charlene was able to handle a full load. He might have put his best waitress in charge of helping Charlene adjust, or he could have done it himself.

Step by step, Frank should have shown Charlene what he expected of her. Slowly and patiently, working at Charlene's pace, Frank could have gradually familiarized her with her duties, first by telling her and then by showing her. People learn by doing things for themselves. Managers or owners must give the new employees plenty of time to get their hands dirty. Let them make mistakes—just be on hand so they learn from their mistakes.

Sometimes a written list indicating all the steps in a specific task can be useful. A waitress's job-breakdown sheet might designate the steps involved in making Irish coffee or filling a guest check. A cook's breakdown sheet might show how to cook a turkey or create a perfect standing rib roast.

Frank should have become better acquainted with Charlene in order to discover her strengths and her weaknesses. Then he would have known how fast she could learn her duties. Some people are faster learners than others. In this age of standardization, managers may regret the differences in their employees, but differences are a fact of life. People progress at their own speed, and threats usually do more harm than good.

To sum it up, instead of throwing Charlene to the wolves, Frank could have:

- explained every detail of the job before she started to work;
- required the other employees to pitch in during the training period;

- personally taught her how to perform her tasks;
- provided a job-breakdown sheet for the more difficult jobs;
- tried to know and understand her.

The new employee should also receive one more thing from the owner: plenty of praise. Understanding, patience, and encouragement go a long way toward making a well-adjusted employee.

EIGHT

Sound People Management

Customer Relations / Employee Relations

THE POWER OF DECISION—IT'S WHY MANY PEOPLE TURN TO small businesses. You are in charge. The authority can be very satisfying, yet a great deal of responsibility rests with the position. What you do as manager affects not only your business, but also the people who work for you.

If you have a chance, go to the library and scan the card catalogue under "Management." It goes on and on and on. There are instruction booklets and massive theoretical studies —all about management. Why? Because management is a principal part of any business, even a small business like yours. As owner you can't ignore your role as manager—unless you want to hire someone else to be your manager. You have to call the shots and try your best to make the correct decision. Careful, incisive management can keep you in business a long time.

This chapter is called "Sound People Management" because it deals with the human elements of the restaurant business. Basically, it covers two groups of people—employees and customers.

CUSTOMER RELATIONS

Technically, you don't manage customers; you manage *for* customers. Every action you make is with the specific purpose of drawing in customers to sell to them. Let's face it, the number of patrons who eat in your restaurant day in and day out, over the course of a year, make or break your restaurant. So, on the surface your goal as manager is simple—merely to maximize the amount of customers.

You've seen how to attract people by the way of advertising and promotion. Now, how do you handle these customers once they are in your restaurant: How do you react to complaints? How do you manage your employees who serve customers? How do you make the patron so pleased he or she wants to come back again and again?

When a customer comes in, the first thing to do is to make him or her feel welcome. Customers have to feel both special and wanted. Nothing is more frustrating to a party of people than standing around behind the "Please wait for the hostess to seat you" sign and watching one waiter after another pass them by without so much as an acknowledgment that they exist. Sure you're busy, sure it's a rush hour and all your help is tied up. You can make a score of legitimate excuses, but excuses don't keep customers. It may be impossible to please everyone all the time, but it's your job as manager to try very hard to do the impossible. If you see a party standing around twiddling their thumbs, go over and explain the situation. Be polite and tell them how long they'll have to wait for a table. They may decide that waiting for a table that night isn't worth it, but the next time they eat out, they won't immediately scratch your restaurant from the list because of poor service.

The basic idea is to be poilte, helpful, and cheerful—even in adversity. And to be successful you must instill these qualities in your waiters, waitresses, counter help, and busboys. The old adage "The customer is always right" still rings true in most cases. You'll discover sooner or later that everyone isn't a sweetheart. There are times that you'll have to cope with unpleasant situations. For example, six big teen-age boys march into your restaurant. They jostle customers, insult waitresses, and start a little food fight at their table. This is a situation that you, the owner and manager, will have to handle on your own. You can't expect your waitress to go on taking abuse from these hoodlums or allow your other customers to be upset. Your first approach should be a quiet, reasonable one. As you take them their food, or even before they receive their food, inform them quietly but firmly to stop horsing around. If they behave, terrific. If they continue to be abusive, politely ask them to leave. If they refuse, you have no alternative to calling the police. But no matter how angry you feel, don't get into a shouting match with a customer. If you call those teen-agers a lot of four-letter names, you will further upset the other patrons and probably provoke the youths into a fight.

Always keep your objective within sight. In the example involving the teen-agers, the manager wanted the situation to remain calm and not to escalate into anything serious. Appearances are also important. Remember, there may be hundreds of eyes on you when you handle a problem customer. Often the other patrons will be on your side if you handle boorishness with an exemplary manner. It may bother you not to trade insults, but you'll look a lot better to your other customers.

What about the picky complainer, the crotchety old man who claims his french fries are soggy or the lettuce under his coleslaw is wilted. Usually customers will have a legitimate complaint, and they should be satisfied immediately. But the same holds true with the professional complainers, too, unfortunately. Don't lose your temper and refuse requests flat out in a hostile tone. Other patrons across the room won't know how sorely you've been tried. All they see is a figure of authority screaming at a sweet little old man.

It takes all kinds, and you'll get your share of the weirdos, but don't lose your cool. Just try to return everything to normal as quickly and quietly as possible.

One suggestion: it is wise to instruct your service personnel never to get into any disagreement with a customer. If the situation looks bad, they should always refer to you. This accomplishes two things. First, it enables you to get involved in any customer-employee problem. You may find your waiter giving the customer a hard time because of some personal problem. In any event, your calming influence will be needed. And second, it removes your help from any potentially dangerous predicament. If a violent drunk sits at one of your tables, you don't want one of your waitresses to try to get him to leave on her own. In fact, it is imperative that you are summoned in any unusual circumstance. If someone suddenly gets ill or collapses, you should be there to try to offer help and avoid lawsuits.

EMPLOYEE RELATIONS

Employee management has received more attention than any other phase of management. Maybe that's because people are the heart of any business, even in the computer industry. There are differing theories about how to treat employees. Years ago managers thought it was best to treat employees like children. They rewarded them when they were good, punished them when they were bad, did their thinking for them, and never asked for an opinion. There are still plenty of managers around today who think like that, but they are a fast-dying breed. Today's manager realizes that employees have to be treated with respect and dignity. Ideally the employee should take a personal interest in the business, be satisfied and happy with his or her position, and feel that he or she has a future.

As manager, you have a great deal of power. You have the power to hire and fire, to threaten, to make life miserable for all of your employees. The employee has two weapons: to quit, or to continue to work but perform little sabotages here and there. It goes without saying that a manager who constantly throws his or her weight around is not going to be very popular. And it naturally follows that employees who aren't happy just won't work as well. In fact, the poor environment will cause high turnover in employees, many sick calls, and plenty of tardiness. Try to run an efficient business with those problems.

So even though you are manager and owner, you still aren't a dictator. You need your employees to run your business, so it only makes sense to treat them as well as possible, in a way that will make them happy to work for you. The idea is to get your employees to work not only for you, but for themselves as well. Try to make them feel that they are contributing to a team effort.

How should you manage your employees? What should you offer and what should you demand? Offer:

- A reasonable salary. Average salaries are low in the restaurant industry, but many employers pay more to get better workers and lower turnover.
- A safe place to work—well ventilated, and no fire trap.
- Pleasant surroundings.
- Patience.
- Objectivity.

Demand from your employees:

- A full day's work.
- That they do their jobs to their best ability.
- That they not steal from you.
- No sabotage.

Management presents unique demands. Working with people under any circumstance produces problems. And you'll have to worry about people who are forced to work often under rush-hour pressure. The more customers your restaurant draws, the better you'll like it, but think about your employees. To them, more customers represent more work, not a walking gold mine. It is not unheard of for employees to actually resent large numbers of customers. If a waitress resents her customers, you've got trouble.

As manager, you need to understand your employees at least as well as your stock. An employee can cost a great deal of money if he or she isn't utilized properly. In addition to wasted labor, employees can cost you money by stealing, goofing off, being careless, and even directly sabotaging your operation. Your actions as people manager determine the actions of your employees to a great extent.

Let's be practical. As a small operator you'll have five or six employees at most. So it is impractical for you to start acting like the chairman of General Motors. In other words, you are never very far removed from your employees—they are also your fellow workers. It is difficult to be a Captain Bligh with people you may have a friendly relationship with. But like any owner-manager in business, you pay their salaries and supply them with benefits for which you (not unreasonably) demand work. Your tasks as a small-restaurant manager are both more and less difficult than those of an impersonal, regal large-corporation manager

First, you are in constant touch with your employees. They are your co-workers. You chat with them during off times, get to know what's on their minds, understand their likes and dislikes, and know how their family life is.

Second, you are in very close personal touch with all your employees. How do you make decisions? Suppose two employees came to you with this problem: Bob the waiter and Sally the waitress both want to handle the table section instead of the counter because tips are higher. Both are good workers, but there is only one section.

BOB: Hey, I really need that section. We're trying to furnish our apartment.

SALLY: I need new clothes for my kid.

BOB: Hey, I'm the breadwinner in my family. I need the money more. Besides, she's not even married, and her ex-husband supports the kid.

SALLY: The last time that bum gave me any money was when he stopped by here for some coffee and left a dime tip.

Both want and feel they need the table section. Make the wrong choice and one may quit. In fact, make the correct choice and one may quit. If the one who wasn't chosen doesn't quit, how do you stay friendly with the one you turned down? You still see him or her every single day. An impersonal manager can direct the lives of thousands of people without coming to grips with the agony a small owner-manager suffers.

You may or may not be able to keep your restaurant on a completely businesslike footing every day. Even so, there really is only one solution: be completely fair. There is a place for friendship in your restaurant, but there is also a place for cool, collected, objective business decisions. It is up to you to make your employees understand this. If they hold your making the right business decisions against you, then there is little you can do.

Try to open all channels of communication. Good communication is the difference between understanding and misunderstanding. As manager you need all the facts before you can make any honest evaluation. Who had seniority, Bob or Sally? Or who deserved to be rewarded for past work?

In a small operation you also can detect uneasiness before it becomes a trend. A large business with several hundred employees may take several months to notice an uncommon rise in labor turnover from a particular department. When a single employee leaves your restaurant, you should pinpoint the reason right away. As you know, employee turnover costs a great deal of money and efficiency. You can't afford to have "trends."

Even before someone quits, there are signs of unhappiness that are easily picked up. How well are your employees working? If they are sullen, resentful, and slow, you've got a problem. Do your employees call in sick often, maybe even a few minutes before work? Do they often come in late? Find out why.

What else should you do as manager? Well, if you read enough books on the subject, you'll come away pretty confused. For example, some authorities claim that it is wrong for you to mix with your employees. And you should never perform "unmanagement-like" tasks, such as pouring coffee, setting tables, washing dishes, and even cooking. Let's be reasonable, however. You run a small place; you have four or five employees. Do you really think that they'll respect you more if you refuse to set a table during a rush period because it is beneath you? A hired manager can afford to be impressed with himself and his position because someone else is paying him a salary. But an owner-manager doesn't have anyone paying him to stand around looking impressive. Sure, someday you may have a gigantic restaurant, and you will be able to afford to roll around in your money while other people pick up the dishes and push the fries, but right now you'll be glad to pitch in at every position—from waiter to dishwasher, from bus boy to maître d'.

This isn't to say that you should make a habit of doing everyone's job. That's just as bad as doing nothing at all. Some owners are always in a hyperactive state—they run around from station to station fixing a salad here, adding salt to a recipe there. This is bad for the employees. One of your goals is to build a trust between you and the people who work for you. Of course, there aren't too many Einsteins who choose to become waitresses and dishwashers, but they have to learn to fly on their own sooner or later. With the amount of work you have to do, you must learn to delegate the proper jobs to the employees you hired to perform them.

NINE

Managing the Money in Your Business

Record-Keeping / The Profit-and-Loss Statement / The Balance Sheet / Cost Percentages / The Importance of Strict Methods of Accounting / Insurance / Planning for the Future

M ONEY—PROFITS—THE REASON YOU'RE IN BUSINESS. There may be a few operators who run restaurants just for the fun of it, but they probably aren't reading this book.

In our society money talks. But to be a success you have to listen. In business, money is the root of all evil only if there isn't enough of it.

RECORD-KEEPING

The problems of being a financial manager are similar to other facets of restaurant management. What does the average small-restaurant owner do wrong? The biggest mistake is laxity. A few records are kept—as few as possible—and only for income tax purposes. Bad mistake. In other chapters you've read about the many ways of losing money through improper purchasing, receiving, storing, etc. We are now at the final stage: the direct handling, accounting, and analyzing of your receipts.

Basically, good money management is like good people management—you must be in tune with what occurs daily around you. Ideally, every cent should be mapped out: what was purchased, when the item was purchased, and what happened to the purchased item. From this money map, analysis should be made and decisions reached. After studying the penny's path, you should know whether or not the money was wisely spent and if you are satisfied with the results of its use.

It may sound easy with a penny, but there are (or should be) thousands of pennies to map through complex mazes. Look at it this way, the final profit from your operation is a little like the spurt of water that shoots out of the nozzle of a leaky garden hose. The more leaks along the hose, the less water pours out the nozzle. Certain holes can't be plugged—the normal, everyday expenses such as food costs, labor costs, and rent— but you can keep these holes from widening. Added to these, there are holes that don't belong in the hose in the first place. Holes like theft, lazy bookkeeping errors, lack of accounting procedures, and poor record-keeping.

Begin with proper bookkeeping. For the first year or two almost all small restaurants make little or no money. And year after year some operations are only marginally successful. Every penny counts. So the first step is to know exactly how your money is working for you. This means detailed, accurate bookkeeping. Most people hate paper work with a passion. It is boring and tedious and oftens appears pointless, as just another burden on the poor taxpayer. Some business people pile receipts, order sheets, and other documents in a heap and hope the accountant can sort things out.

Although you should have an accountant, it is a mistake not to be familiar with your own financial records. Your financial information is the pulse of your business. If you are maintaining proper books, you are keeping a finger on that pulse. You know when it's strong and when it's weak. In fact, your financial statements can forecast a part of the future. But you have to work at it.

The primary rule is: accurately document everything—all purchases, all expenses, and all sales. This daily information is written in your journal. Make your entries easy to read, because the journal chronologically documents all transactions. From the journal, the daily information is itemized on ledger sheets. The ledger sheet indicates transactions for a specific period of time (usually a month) under specific account headings. Payroll, sales, and purchases all may have their own ledger sheet.

But the journal and the ledger are only the raw materials. It is up to you to make sense out of the rows upon rows of numbers. There are two basic tools: the profit-and-loss statement and the balance sheet.

The Profit-and-Loss Statement

Your records must tell you exactly what shape your business is in. How successful are you? A profit-and-loss statement is a useful business barometer; it simply tells you how much money your restaurant made or lost. It is a summary of money received during the course of business and how much money was paid in the form of expenses to keep the restaurant running.

PROFIT-AND-LOSS STATEMENT

	Amount	Percentages
Food sales	$120,000	100%
Cost of food	48,000	40
Gross income	$ 72,000	60%
Controllable Expenses		
Payroll	$ 36,000	30%
Employee benefits	4,800	4
Advertising	2,400	2
Operating expenses	6,000	5
Utilities	2,400	2
Administrative	3,600	3
Maintenance	1,200	1
Total controllable expenses	$ 56,400	47%
Profit before rent	$ 15,600	13%
Rent	6,000	5
Profit before depreciation	$ 9,600	8%
Depreciation	1,200	1
Net income before taxes	$ 8,400	7%

A profit-and-loss statement should be drawn up on a regular basis—at least every three months. By studying the changes from one accounting period to another you can tell how business is progressing.

The Balance Sheet

The profit-and-loss statement is a great tool for determining your hard money figures, but you need another tool to discover how much your business is really worth. This is where the balance sheet comes in. The balance sheet is essentially a summing up of the ledger. It lists your total assets and liabilities and includes such items as property value, depreciation, inventories —everything that you have tied up in the business. It also includes everything you owe, such as outstanding loans.

BALANCE SHEET

Current Assets

Cash on hand and in bank	$ 8,000	
Merchandise inventory (food and supplies)	3,000	
Prepaid insurance, taxes	1,500	
Total current assets	$12,500	$12,500

Fixed Assets

Real Estate—Land		$ 9,000
Real Estate—Building:		
Original cost	$32,000	
Less depreciation	1,500	
		$30,500
Furniture, fixtures, and equipment		
Original cost	$ 6,000	
Less depreciation	300	
		$ 5,700
TOTAL ASSETS		$57,700

Current Liabilities

Accounts payable	$16,000	
Notes payable	$ 8,000	
Total current liabilities		$24,000
Long-term debt		$11,000
Capital		$22,700
TOTAL LIABILITIES AND CAPITAL		$57,700

COST PERCENTAGES

Another useful tool in food operations is the cost percentages. This is a simple but useful guide to certain expenses (usually food). All you have to do is add up your sales total for a particular time period—say, a week or a month—and then add up the food cost for the same period. Now divide the sales by the food cost and you have your percentage.

You are left with a figure that indicates how big a hunk your food costs take from your gross sales. Food cost is the largest expense the restaurant operator has to deal with. By checking the food-cost percentage over a period of time, you can see how current cost compares with that in previous time periods. If you discover the food cost skyrocketing in relation to sales, you can try to assess why. It may be a normal seasonal fluctuation, or it might be an indicator that your menu is too heavily stacked with low-profit items or that your prices are out of line. If inflation has hit the raw food materials, but you haven't adjusted your prices, it will be reflected in higher food-cost percentages. It's possible your chef has been botching the job—or even worse, an employee may be stealing food.

Similarly, you can figure out a percentage for any facet of your business. Food is the biggest headache in any restaurant, although labor is coming up fast on the inside track. A simple percentage won't tell exactly what the problem is, but it will indicate whether or not you have a problem.

But remember, you must collect accurate information to begin with, and it must be analyzed scrupulously or you might as well forget about the whole thing.

THE IMPORTANCE OF STRICT METHODS OF ACCOUNTING

An unwary owner is looking for trouble in the restaurant business. There are too many ways employees can steal an owner blind. John didn't think record-keeping was important. For years he didn't bother with duplicate checks. He was a trusting soul who let the waiters and waitresses make oral orders to the kitchen.

Then he discovered the fleecing he was getting. One night Sarah, a trusted waitress who had worked for John nearly three years, served a deluxe steak-and-lobster dinner to a personal friend who was a regular customer. John had often noted with pleasure the expensive dinners this customer always ordered. He was a few feet away from the cashier when the customer paid his total bill of $3.50 for his meal. His total should have been a little over $20 with tax included. Suddenly, John turned into a very suspicious person. Who was the crook? The customer obviously was in on the deception, but who was his partner—the waitress or the cashier? This at least was easily solved. After the customer left, John strolled over to the cashier and took a stack of guest checks. The customer's was on the top. It read "chopped sirloin dinner—$3.50." Sarah the waitress was the culprit. She had written one thing and orally ordered something else. And this had been going on for months.

This is just one type of theft, and it should be obvious how to prevent it. There should be duplicates of each order check— one for the kitchen and one for the customer. Each check number should correspond to another.

The point is, however, that there should be a strict method of accounting, both for the service personnel and the kitchen personnel. Watch both money and stocks like a hawk. It is easy to lose money through the front and the back door and possibly a couple of open windows.

The small-restaurant owner must never be under the impression that his or her business is "too small" to bother with details like good bookkeeping and analysis of financial records. Proper record-keeping and accounting is vital for any business. Your records not only protect you against theft and waste; they also tell you when you've done something right. Essentially your financial tools do three things for you:

(1) They present you with an accurate record of your business. (This is important if you want to get a loan— just try it without any records.)

(2) You have the means to determine exactly how well your restaurant is succeeding.

(3) Past profit-and-loss statements, balance sheets, and percentages can be used to forecast future business trends. By studying all the past data, you can chart a smooth course for your business future.

INSURANCE

Two hours after the owner of the Grillerie had closed his restaurant, he got a call from the local fire department. His beautiful restaurant had gone up in smoke.

At the Eastern Palace, a local gang smashed in the front window, vandalized the restaurant's interior, and looted everything that wasn't nailed down.

Joe's Chili House put out their special mystery sauce as usual. But the main mystery in the sauce that day was the presence of salmonella germs. Sixteen patrons got very sick and then very angry; their lawyers sued. The mystery was cleared up when it was discovered that the cook had not taken proper sanitary precautions after using the bathroom.

Each case is different, but any or all can happen to you. You must have protection. If you own a restaurant, you know that certain types of insurance are mandatory—workman's compensation, for instance.

What policies should you have? Fire and liability are the two most necessary. The dangers of fire and injury are very high in the restaurant business. Over the years there have been thousands of restaurant fires, from small, contained grease fires to raging infernos that have wiped out entire city blocks. And the risk of a customer getting hurt on your premise exists. Whether a drunken customer falls out a window or a sober one contracts food poisoning, it is best to be protected. Otherwise, one lawsuit can wipe you out.

Look into your own needs very carefully before you obtain coverage. There are two problems: too little insurance and too much insurance. It is vital that you are fully protected against disasters, such as fire or explosion. But coverage of an item like your plate glass window might prove to be more expensive than it's worth. Determine your needs, how much you can afford to spend, and what it will take to make you feel secure. Discuss your insurance needs with a broker or a number of brokers. Know what it will take to keep your operation humming along in case of a calamity.

PLANNING FOR THE FUTURE

No restaurant can afford to stand still. Even Mother Marge's Down Home Cooking has to think about the future. Few businesses are static. Too many things affect them. And restaurants are among the most easily affected businesses—by growing competition, shifting population and economic centers, changing tastes.

One of the most difficult changes to handle, strangely enough, is success. What should the small-restaurant owner do if he makes it big? The first thing that pops into mind is expansion —maybe starting a chain, or even developing a franchise. But change is always fraught with danger. The small-restaurant owner must know himself and his restaurant's capabilities. Maybe an Armenian restaurant is an unqualified success in a metropolis like New York City, but how would an Armenian chain do in the Midwest. In some small restaurants the character of the owner is what creates success. If the owner buys two other places, the personal touch that brought in the original customers disappears. And it's always dangerous to try to do too much at once; many business failures result from over-expansion.

There are also many incredible success stories. All the gigantic fast-food chains today started with single restaurants, most of them rather humble roadside stands. Ingenuity, good products, and very hard work created the success stories. Many large restaurant owners began with tiny restaurants. They started small and bought progressively larger and larger places.

First, what do you want? Some small-restaurant owners remain small because they're satisfied. They don't want the extra headache. But many small-restaurant owners have a vision. They dream about McDonald-style chains or large high-class restaurants like the Four Seasons or the Brown Derby.

The most profitable way to expand, enlarge, or diversify is to maintain a tight rein on the finances. Keep in close touch with your banker. You'll be surprised at the number of doors open to you when you succeed. And a banker who has watched you grow—with healthy skepticism slowly changing to admiration—is in a position to further you along the path with loans.

The best restaurants are exciting, ever-changing enterprises. The good restaurant owner can handle all the changes that come his or her way. In fact, the challenge keeps the interest alive. A creative business person can adapt to and utilize any new fortune. It takes a little verve and a lot of nerve, but the smallest restaurant in the hands of the proper business person can skyrocket. So good luck, and shoot for the moon.

TEN

The Law
and Your Business

The Importance of Knowing the Law / Taxes

THE IMPORTANCE OF KNOWING THE LAW

EVER GET THE FEELING THAT SOMEONE IS LOOKING OVER your shoulder? You should if you're in the restaurant business. There are laws and regulations covering almost everything you do, in and out of the kitchen. And it pays to know exactly what the laws in your particular community are.

In some states you must provide a locker area for employees. Other states demand special equipment—a three-compartment sink for washing, sterilizing, and rinsing pots and pans. And a law that can really cause trouble is the truth-in-merchandising law. One restaurant owner went a little overboard in creating his menu; he claimed that he served giant, fresh strawberries swimming in thick cream. The truth was that the thick cream was plain milk. So the owner was fined—and he also got the bad publicity of being known as someone who didn't serve what the menu said he should serve. Some restaurants make even smaller slips. For example, serving margarine and calling it butter. But don't fall into the habit of calling margarine butter in your restaurant, because in some states it can lead to a fine.

Sanitary regulations are probably the most common, and perhaps the most important. Without strict enforcement of sanitary codes, the consumer could be in serious trouble. You may groan at some of the laws, but they are for your good as well as that of the people who eat your food. Let's face it, a dining room full of poisoned people would not be the best for business.

Most laws are on the books to protect consumers, not to discourage the business man or woman. But frustration and discouragement will be the lot of any restaurant owner who doesn't pay full attention to the law.

If you built your restaurant from scratch, you learned a great deal about the law. Plans for your restaurant had to be submitted to local officials for approval. If anything was a whisker out of place, you heard it well in advance.

But what about the restaurant owner who buys an existing restaurant? Again, it's like buying a used car. If the prospective buyer is wise, he gets in touch with the local office of the Health Department and uses an official like his personal mechanic. The official notes the number and kind of violations and lets the prospective buyer discover how much more money is going to be needed to correct those violations.

Laws and regulations change all the time, and you certainly can expect more to come in this age of consumer activism. As an owner of a small restaurant, you must know all about the laws and regulations that apply to you. Remember, just because you don't know that a certain law is on the books doesn't mean that law can't affect you. The old cliché "ignorance of the law is no excuse" really is true.

You can keep abreast of all the new laws by joining a local restaurant trade organization. Another good idea is to participate in your local government. Know what they plan before they do it. But no matter how you do it, you must know all the outside forces that can significantly affect your business. It doesn't make sense to pay fines or receive adverse publicity when a little extra time spent on your part will keep you informed.

TAXES

An even bigger headache than laws and regulations is taxation. Although we can be sure of death and taxes, it's hard to choose which is least welcome.

No matter what size your restaurant is, you'll need an accountant to set up your tax structure. The average restaurant owner has a multitude of different taxes to pay. You need an accountant to outline all the existing taxes for you and to show you how to document and pay them.

Some taxes vary from state to state—for example, the rate of sales tax. Some states don't even bother levying sales tax on meals. And in addition to sales and federal taxes, your local community may have a special tax for you.

Then there are the payroll deductions you'll have to make from your employees' paychecks. The percentage of these withholdings varies from state to state, too.

And of course, you'll have to pay federal income tax (probably state too) and real estate taxes if you own your own restaurant.

PART TWO

Starting Out

ELEVEN

What to Consider When Starting Out

The Nature of the Restaurant Business / Drawbacks and Satisfactions / Your Type of Restaurant / Franchises / Family Operations / The Value of Experience

THE NATURE OF THE RESTAURANT BUSINESS

IF OWNING A RESTAURANT IS STILL A DREAM TO YOU, BEGIN here. There's much to learn before you submerge yourself in the mysterious business of purchasing food or managing employees.

Any small business demands meticulous care and planning. Restaurants are no exception—in fact, planning is more important for a restaurant than most other businesses. There are many failures in this industry, because running a restaurant appears deceptively easy. Everyone has eaten in a restaurant, and from where the customer sits the hard work is hidden. How many people have you heard say: "When I retire I plan to take it easy. Maybe I'll open up a nice quiet little restaurant and work when I feel like it." Don't believe it! Just because your outdoor barbecue for fifteen succeeds or you can whip up ten courses for twenty people at a dinner party, don't fall prey to your guests' well-meaning suggestions that you should open a restaurant.

The two roads to disaster in the restaurant business are: (1) the belief that all there is to the business is cooking food and taking money; and (2) the belief that a restaurant can be run like a factory, forgetting that it is a service industry. Look at it this way. A restaurant owner must be a business person to handle

- purchasing
- salary
- taxes
- loans
- insurance
- profit-and-loss statement
- uniform portion control
- inventory
- recipe standardization
- local laws and ordinances
- advertising and promotion

In addition the owner must be people-oriented as well and understand how to deal with

- customer complaints
- employee problems
- decor
- customer relations
- unions
- the restaurant's image

And if the restaurant has an owner-chef, he or she must be creative and able to handle tremendous pressures, especially during rush hours.

Are there special qualities the prospective small-restaurant owner should possess? Certainly, it would be helpful if he or she were a genius, a workaholic, independently wealthy, a Wall Street wizard, an actor, and a politician. But if you had all these qualities you'd probably run for president or maybe consent to being king.

Seriously, if you are reasonably intelligent and unafraid of hard work and long hours, you have the basics. Sure, it would be wonderful if you were a Harvard MBA and a Cordon Bleu graduate, but there is one quality that will help you more than anything else: a *desire to succeed*. If you have your heart set on creating a vital, moneymaking operation and are willing to dig, probe, plan, and learn all you can about the restaurant business, you'll have a good shot. If you have a little capital and a lot of common sense, your determination and motivation will do the rest.

DRAWBACKS AND SATISFACTIONS

First, are you sure you really want to own a small restaurant? Along with the satisfactions there are lots of headaches and heartaches, including:

- Long hours, especially when you're starting out. Figure on arriving early and closing late—after all your employees are long gone.
- Unexpected expenses—skyrocketing equipment prices, high labor costs, big rent bills, huge utility payments. And don't forget that you and your family have to live, too. You may have severe money problems for the first few months or years.
- A demanding clientele expects high quality; substandard food and poor service will put you out of business, unless you own the only restaurant in the middle of the Mojave desert.
- A wide range of responsibilities. As owner you're wearing a sign saying "The Buck Stops Here." If your cook poisons ten people, they sue you, not him or her. You get the blame because it's your restaurant, your success, your failure; nobody else—just you.

There are these satisfactions:

- Satisfaction number one is that it's all yours. You may take the blame, but you also get the credit. There is that wonderful sense of independence from superiors (of course, you have to bow to the desire of your customers, but they aren't really bosses). It's your business, your baby, your island.
- There are dozens of opportunities to express individual creativity in the restaurant business—different menus, advertising, promotion, themes, formats. The smart restaurant owner experiments and improvises. He or she is con-

stantly trying something new, something that will make the restaurant more attractive and draw in more customers, which creates a sense of excitement.

- And the great satisfaction of doing a good job in a service industry. Seeing regular customers come back again and again gives you a fantastic feeling of pride and accomplishment. When you work hard for a giant corporation, and really keep your nose to the grindstone, the company gets the credit—not you. Maybe you do, by way of a raise, receive recognition from a higher echelon within the company. But who outside the company knows how hard you work? All your hard work goes for the betterment of the company. You're a cog, perhaps a superior one, but still a cog. If you own your own restaurant, you're the wheel, not just a cog. In addition to granting yourself a bigger salary and banking a larger share of the profits, you have the satisfaction of knowing that a restaurant reviewer or a happy customer is complimenting you when they say nice things about your place. By extension, your restaurant is you. Your mind conceived its existence, and your hard work keeps it running.

Still interested? Good. Enthusiasm is important; knowing the enemy, however, is vital. Go to Chapter One and answer, honestly, all the questions from the SBA. They cover the entire range of business areas you should familiarize yourself with before you plunge into running a small business. You can never know too much about the business. If you don't keep your eyes open, something will hit you in the head. Running a small restaurant is like tightrope walking. Increase your chances by keeping the rope taut.

YOUR TYPE OF RESTAURANT

What type of establishment is best for you? There are two factors to consider: what do you want, and what can you afford? Restaurants come in different shapes, sizes, and forms. You have the whole gamut to choose from—roadside snack trucks selling aromatic hot dogs and sauerkraut, doughnut bars catering to the lunchtime crowds, or small, cozy restaurants with dim lights and plush decorations that attract executives for lunch and after-theater patrons for dinner.

Popular small restaurants include the fast-food or specialty establishments. A bare-bones, limited-equipment operation serving a limited menu may be just what will fit your budget. The philosophy of the fast-food stand is to serve the highest number of customers possible in the shortest time. The low check average is offset by the low-budget decor and fast turnover. But just because fast-food stands are popping up like mushrooms, don't make the mistake Charlie H. made. He opened a combination fried-chicken and hamburger stand beside a well-traveled highway. Unfortunately, along this same stretch of road his neighbors were McDonald's, Burger Chef, Burger King, and the Kentucky Colonel. Charlie discovered his single stand was competing with the big boys for the same pool of customers. Although his chicken prices were competitive with Kentucky Fried Chicken, his reputation and advertising budget wasn't. And he couldn't offer a burger with the appeal of a Big Mac or a Whopper. Charlie wasn't shut out, but business wasn't good enough to keep him going. The competition, in this case, was too heavy. The number of customers couldn't support that many fast-food restaurants.

Charlie might have done better if he had decided to compete indirectly, to offer fast food with a little more imagination and flare to separate his place from the competitors'. But the franchises that are nationwide command the larger share of the business.

FRANCHISES

Speaking of franchises, it is possible that you may want to go that route instead of opening up an independent place. Franchised fast-food restaurants are a part of the American way of life. Who hasn't licked his or her fingers after a bucket of extra crispy? And McDonalds' billions of burgers are sliding down a lot of American throats.

Some restaurateurs turn up their noses at these franchises. They consider them to be like filling stations for people—drive in, gas up, and go away in the space of ten or fifteen minutes. But the moneymaking potential of these restaurants is nothing to turn up your nose at. More and more Americans are eating on the run, and they're the ones the franchises cater to.

What exactly is a franchise? A franchise is a developed business that the owner or owners decide to form into a corporation; he sells individual, local outlets on a state or nationwide basis. The seller is the franchiser and the buyer is the franchisee. There are the usual fast-food, limited-menu types of eatery that sell chicken, hamburgers, or roast beef sandwiches; there are those that offer a family-style menu, and there are franchised steak outlets.

Is the franchise for you? No matter what you have read, franchises are not easy money or get-rich-quick treasure troves. A franchise takes just as much hard work as any other new business. The advantage of the franchise is that you have a built-in identity. The public knows you. The parent corporation provides advertising to draw in the public, but this is not a matter of good will; you contribute a certain percentage of earnings to cover such costs.

Your franchise sells exactly what other such franchises sell across the country. This is a plus and a minus. The franchise insists on such tight regulations because the public responds favorably to uniformity. When a customer walks into a McDonald's, he or she knows that the Big Mac is two all-beef patties, etc., etc. The special sauce is the same in Des Moines as in Los Angeles. In short, the customer knows what to expect. What would happen if Des Moines didn't offer special sauce, or Philadelphia decided that sesame-seed buns were too extravagant? The franchise system would cease to be the same business if each franchisee went his own way. If Boston's McDonald's sold Italian sausages and Cleveland's sold chicken, there would be no image to sell, there would be no franchise.

But the rigidity of the menu and the very strict guidelines can be stultifying. You serve the same menu day in and day out. You have no say in the advertising. You just contribute your percentage and hope for the best. In a franchise you also have something that many small-business men and women try to get away from: an immediate superior.

There are good, reputable franchise organizations with many years of experience and solid expertise. There are also franchises that have stayed in business a year or less, collected the franchisees' fees, and skipped town. How do you tell the crooks from the real McCoy?

- Check, recheck, and check again. Dig long, hard, and deep into the prospective franchise. Even if it is a big-name, household-word establishment, make sure you know and agree with all your obligations.
- Talk to several.franchisees. See if they have any gripes. How satisfied are they? Did the parent company provide enough expertise, or did it leave them to fend for themselves? Do they make as much as they expected?
- Look at the books, especially in the case of new or little-known franchises. Don't fall for the honeyed sale of an expert salesman. Get the cold, hard, dollar-and-cents facts.
- See if the better-business bureau has had any complaints. If they have, find out why.

In addition to discovering whether or not the franchise is on the level, look over all the legal ramifications. If you aren't satisfied, how hard would it be to pull out of the business? Will the parent company buy back the business? What obligations do you have if you want to sell your business? Read the contract, every line. Don't take anything for granted, and make no assumptions. No matter what the salesman *says* that the franchiser will do, don't believe it unless it is in the contract. You'll discover that a salesman may promise to babysit your kids and shine your shoes—until you sign. After your signature is on the contract, memories fade fast. Demand what you want in black and white. Accept no oral commitments. None! The time for demands is before the contract is signed. Afterward is too late.

FAMILY OPERATIONS

One serious problem new restaurant owners face is the strain the long hours place on family life. A way to avoid this problem is to run a family operation. It's not a new idea; in fact, 19 percent of American restaurants are family-operated. Ethnic restaurants have applied this organization for years. For example, in some small Chinese restaurants the husband may be the chef, the wife may handle the cash register, one son and his wife may wait on tables, and another son may wash dishes.

Togetherness like this works well at times and poorly at other time, but husbands and wives certainly should think about running the family business together. Since traditional roles are changing anyway, take advantage of it. A husband-and-wife team can run a restaurant more efficiently than a single person with divided responsibilities. The husband may be the head chef and handle the food-related side of the business while the wife does the accounting and bookkeeping, or vice versa. Do whatever works for you.

THE VALUE OF EXPERIENCE

People open restaurants for different reasons. Some decide that they can operate a restaurant because they've spent years as chefs, waitresses, or general managers for other owners. They know and like the restaurant industry. Other people open restaurants because they think that it's a good business to be in or other people have persuaded them that they should open one up. Often, the second group does not really know what they are getting into. Some experience might have given them more confidence or better prepared them.

For example: Michael quit college after two years. He was bored and wanted something to do. His parents gave him the remainder of the money saved for his college tuition and told him he was on his own. Since he had been going to an expensive school, this was a tidy sum. But what was he to do with it? He toyed with the idea of starting a business, and decided a small restaurant in his home town would be perfect. He nosed around, asked local restaurant owners, and even hung around the kitchens. He scouted possible locations and checked financial angles. He found a good spot that was within his means. But there was one problem—Michael. Hanging around kitchens hadn't taught him everything. He was unsure of sinking his savings into the venture, especially after he read the mortality-rate statistics of new restaurants. Luckily, he decided he needed more experience. So he left his money in the bank and found a job as an assistant chef in a restaurant similar to the type he wanted to open. The salary he was earning wasn't important, but the experience he was getting was. After six months he felt secure about opening his own business, but he stayed on for a year anyway to smooth out the rough edges. It was the best-spent year of his life. At the end of a year, he collected his money and rented a building.

Was Michael successful? Even after all this planning, it's too early to tell, but he did display sound thinking. His chances of being successful are much greater than they would have been if he had thrown his money into a venture in which he had no experience.

Should everyone take a job in a restaurant before they open one? For many people it is neither practical nor possible. But it is a good idea to familiarize yourself with as many details of the business as possible. If you can't follow Michael's example, an excellent way of preparing yourself is to take courses from local universities or community colleges. Look at their continuing-education programs. Often they offer many business-related courses, including some right in your field.

It's all part of getting that edge. You want to be successful, more successful than your competitors. The more you know and the better you feel about the business, the better chance you'll have for getting that edge that guarantees your success.

TWELVE

Financing

How Much? / Where to Get It / Banks / Trade Credit / Time Payments / Partners / Small Business Administration / Other Sources

Two big questions must be answered before your restaurant dreams can be realized: (1) How much money do you need? (2) Where will you get it?

HOW MUCH?

The "how much" question can't be answered until you have (1) decided on what type of operation to build; and (2) done an in-depth study of what's available, equipment costs, and down payments. It is vital to work out the major details before you start your quest for funds, because in these days of tight money, finding sufficient backing can be as exhausting as searching for the Holy Grail.

While you are trying to discover how much your venture will cost, start thinking about the other side of the coin—what do you think your business will gross in sales volume? This is important. If you think that a medium-priced, small French restaurant with three waiters, six bus boys, five chefs, elaborate sterling silver tableware, and ten tables will make money, think again. Your sales have to be large enough to cover your investment and make you a little money. If, before you start, you discover that the setup just won't generate enough sales to justify your business, then you'll just have to scrap the idea or modify it.

ESTIMATED SALES AND PROFITS

A. Analysis of potential sales
   Total seats (30) $\times$ estimated turnover (1.5) =
   45 dinners per day and 270 per week.
   Estimated average check = $6
   Total dinner sales per week (270 $\times$ 6) = $1,620

B. Projection of costs
   Cost of food (estimated at 40% of sales) $ 648
   Cost of labor (minimum)
      1 Chef $200
      2 Waitresses   120
      1 Dishwasher   90
      Total estimated labor cost per week $ 410
   All other operating costs (estimated)   200
      Total estimated operating costs $1,258
   Taxes, interest, and amortization of mortgage   100
      Total estimated cost per week $1,358

C. Projection of potential profit (before owner's
   compensation for his own services) (per week) $ 262

Remember to be realistic in your figures. Someday your restaurant may be the talk of two continents and gross over $5 million, but the overwhelming probability is that your first few months will be very tight. Good, objective planning will prepare you for those cash vacuums that suck up every extra penny.

WHERE TO GET IT

OK, you've settled on the type of restaurant, you've drawn up a list of costs, and you have a fair idea how much capital you need to get it all off the ground. The big question is, Where do you get the money?

Not an easy question. You may have a wonderful idea, but if you can't put up a chunk of the money yourself, then few commercial institutions will give you more than the time of day. Therefore, source number one is what you can raise yourself before you try to get a loan. This money is your equity capital, the money you plan to use to start your business. Where do you find it?

- Your own nest egg. Many people save for years before they buy their own business.
- Relatives. If you have a rich uncle or brother, see if they'd like to invest in your restaurant. A word of caution, dealing with relatives can be tricky. Not too many will drag you to court if you default, but plenty of them will be happy to tell you how to run your business.
- Friends. Friends and relatives are alike, except friends of the fair-weather variety may not stay friends for long if you go against their whims.
- Business contacts. They may be willing to invest if you offer a good chance of success.

It is important in each case to handle the investments on a strictly business footing. Just because you always were Aunt Molly's favorite nephew doesn't mean Auntie Molly expects nothing in return for her loan or investment. Figure out percentages or interest and pay promptly. If nothing else, it's good practice because sooner or later you'll be dealing with professionals.

Banks

After relatives and friends, the first place you'll think of turning to is to your friendly local bank. After all, they're in the business of lending money, and since that's what you're after, there should be no problem. Unfortunately, it just ain't so. Restaurants have a bad reputation—remember the statistics! And if you don't have any restaurant experience, don't expect your banker to contribute to what he thinks may be a lost cause.

But you should have a good business relationship with a commercial bank anyway. While they don't look with favor on fledgling restaurateurs, they are impressed with successful concerns. When you offer proof that the first big wind didn't blow you away, then they may want to sit down and do some real talking. This can be especially helpful after you have made your name and want to expand or remodel.

A banker also is a source of advice. He or she may caution you about buying a restaurant in a bad area. A good bank should be familiar with the state of local businesses.

If you do have restaurant experience, if you can supply a major chunk of the initial outlay; and if you have some collateral, then a bank may be quite willing to offer some form of loan—with a few conditions. You must satisfy them that you're an excellent risk. So be prepared to answer questions like:

- What is your net worth?
- What are your outstanding debts?
- What income do you expect your business to do?
- What percentage of total sales will cover overhead expenses?
- What items of expense will you show?
- What will the cost of carrying a normal inventory be?

A banker isn't going to give you a dime if you can't offer some proof of what you are talking about, so go prepared.

Trade Credit

In addition to normal loans, you'll quickly discover that trade credit will be available. Trade credit is essentially postponing payment on either shipment or supplies as long as possible. By the time payment is demanded you should be making money from the materials. But trade credit can be costly, because if you have the money to pay on purchase, you'll receive a substantial discount.

Time Payments

Restaurant equipment dealers also will make arrangements to sell ovens, dishwashers, etc. with 25 to 35 percent down and to finance the balance. This is a nice workable arrangement as long as neither party abuses it. A hustling dealer may link credit to the purchase of more equipment than you need. When the dealer says in a loud voice that he'll allow credit if you take his newest-model walk-in freezer and a microwave oven, *and* a steam table, stop and think. The last thing you need is a big hunk of unused machinery gathering dust while you pay for it through the nose. Don't forget, you're not through paying after you've made the down payment. Think about the months and years ahead, and don't get in over your head. The salesman always has the option of coming back and wheeling out his nice shiny ovens and freezers if you don't pay.

Partners

If you find that with loans, investments, trade credit, and time payments you still can't make ends meet, you may want a partner. In a partnership you sell part of the business and take on an individual who is as much an owner as you are. Your partner assumes both liability and a hunk of your business. This means that he or she has the right to make decisions concerning the handling of the business. This can be a sticky point with many partnerships. Suddenly you aren't alone. You may think the restaurant needs two more bus boys, but your partner thinks that the payroll is too high as it is. Prepare to argue and then compromise. Of course, a partner could be a great asset, too. You may be excellent as a cook but a little uncertain when it comes to bookkeeping. If your partner could assume responsibility over one area of the business while you ran the other, you might enjoy smooth operation.

Small Business Administration

If you discover that you just can't borrow enough money from private sources, there still is hope. The Small Business Administration will supply loans to prospective businessmen who can't get the money anywhere else. Of course you have to prove that you can't find the money—two banks must deny you loans and you must show that you're unable to sell part ownership in the business and that other private and government sources won't help you.

Certain businesses are off limits to the SBA. Restaurants are ineligible if more than 50 percent of their sales is from alcoholic beverages. Be prepared to go into your personal finances in depth. And then don't be surprised if the loan takes a while to go through.

Other Sources

There are other sources of aid:

- Small-business investment companies (SBICs). These are private firms supported by the SBA. They offer long-term loans based on some form of collateral.
- Credit unions.
- Veterans' organizations.
- State and local development companies.
- Landlord improvements. (Sometimes it makes sense to go to the source. Some landlords will furnish all restaurant facilities in return for a percentage of gross sales.)

For more information in this area see Egon W. Loffel. *Financing Your Business*. New York: McKay, 1977.

THIRTEEN

How to Use
the Money

*Rent, Buy, or Build? / Picking the Right Location / Buying
Equipment*

A T THIS POINT, YOU KNOW HOW TO GET FUNDS, YOU KNOW
what type of restaurant is right for you, and you're ready
to move. What do you look for? By this time you should have
looked at ads (under business opportunities), talked to real
estate salesmen (some firms specialize in restaurants—this
shows what kind of market there is), and nosed around in general. You know for a fact that there seem to be hundreds of
solid offerings on the market. But this is where you should use
every ounce of your judgment. You have to pick a place that is
right for you and your business.

You have a number of options.

- Do you plan to take over an existing restaurant?
- Do you plan extensive remodeling?
- Do you want to build everything from scratch?
- Do you want to rent a space in a new shopping mall?

Maybe you've discovered the perfect building, everything seems
great—only it's located fifty miles away from any population
center.

Remember:

- You have to stay within your budget. If you overspend, it
  might be fatal.

- You must keep a very tight rein on any improvements, re-decorating, or remodeling. Make sure it all fits in with local ordinances.
- The same applies if you build from scratch, only you also have to pay attention to annoyances such as zoning laws.
- Make absolutely certain about the location. How does it stack up now? How will it be in the future? Try to look at past developments in the community and project to the future. In five years' time will your classy French restaurant be located in the heart of a slum or warehouse district? If you slip up on location, you can prepare yourself for a slow, lingering, but certain business death.

RENT, BUY, OR BUILD?

Let's look at these concerns more closely. First, should you rent, buy, or build? For everyone with a tight budget, building is almost certainly out of the question. Anyone planning on building his restaurant has to pick a suitably zoned area and pay premium prices for the land. Then there are the building costs. Going by past inflation in the construction industry, you won't get off very cheap. Then there is the time factor. If a strike doesn't hit, you may have everything ready within a year or so. So you must take into account how you're going to survive while the restaurant is being built.

There is a partial solution for certain prospective restaurant owners who do want their own building, and fast—pre-fabs. These are not inexpensive either, and in some areas they don't satisfy zoning laws, but they are a possibility for the future. A Hong Kong builder offers a fully prefabricated Chinese Restaurant down to the chopsticks and food supply, and he claims that he can erect one anywhere in the world within a few months. As pre-fabricated housing evolves, there probably will be many opportunities such as this one for specialized establishments. On balance, though, the practical solution to housing your restaurant is rental of an existing premises.

Check your local newspaper. Try looking under "Business Opportunities." "Restaurants for Sale" takes up a sizable print area, and plenty of ads look good, if not downright exciting.

LUNCHEONETTE Nice clientele, business location, very profitable. Good hrs, no Sundays. Attractive selling price.

Restaurant & bar for Sale. Excel Loc. Newly decorated, Gross approx. $225M yearly. Price $85,000. $25,000 cash.

Gross weekly $5500. Long Is. Residential & business area. Cash + terms.

COFFEE SHOP very busy location. Long lease. Low rent, low cash, $4500 per week income.

DINER By the Beach—good loc, remodeled, fully equipped—good deal.

ELEGANT RESTAURANT,

ACTIVE, PRESTIGE LOCATION Attractive decor for gracious dining. Fully eqpd—operating cond. 15 yr lease. Small cash down. Advantageous long-term financing.

Restaurant. Leasing because of illness. New interior. Seats 60. $750 per month plus security. Negotiable. Min 2 yrs.

Bar/Lounge/restaurant $72,500 includes RE/equipment/furnishings.

DINER FOR LEASE or Sale w/dining rm, seats 80, fully eqpd. well establ business on cor acres, ample parking. Can convert easily to any type food operation.

Buying a going concern is one way to enter the restaurant business on your feet. There is no long waiting period while you buy equipment, have it installed, go through the motions of hiring people, etc. And the operating restaurant comes complete with patrons. You'll be doing business from the minute you sign the papers. Look at those sample ads—$1,500 weekly gross, $2,000 weekly gross, and only a few dollars down for a beautiful restaurant in a beautiful, busy location. What more could you want? Why is the owner selling?

The balloon just burst. Don't forget those statistics on the number of restaurants that fail each year. An owner finds himself going out of business, he wants to dump the lemon as soon as possible. How does he advertise? "Low-grossing restaurant with lazy employees, obsolete equipment, in need of extensive repairs, closed on occasion by Department of Health and located in the heart of a slum; for sale—cheap?" No. He writes one of those nice ads: "High-grossing city restaurant with excellent equipment located in the heart of bustling community.

Buy this restaurant, it's a great way of life. Must sacrifice because of health. $15,000 down." Then a prospective buyer walks in, one who hasn't checked the market, and sees a spotless dining room and shiny equipment. The owner pitches a spiel, steers him away from the books, gets all his friends to drop by that night to show how crowded the place gets . . . and before you know it another newcomer is in the restaurant business. Unfortunately for him, he's trying to stay afloat with one hundred pounds of dead weight tied around his neck.

Not all going concerns are bad. In fact, many are extremely good buys. Sam J. wanted to open a small seafood restaurant on the Connecticut shore. He spent several weeks going up the shore from Greenwich to Norwalk, and he discovered that several existing restaurants were for sale. After another week he narrowed the field down to three possibilities. These three were within his price range, they satisfied his standard for size and locations, and preliminary checking indicated that they were legitimate businesses. Then Sam went in and asked the hard questions. Here's a sample list from the SBA:

- **From the Real Estate Broker or Landlord:**
  How long has he known the client?
  Has he ever eaten in the restaurant?
  Why does the owner wish to sell?
  Will the lease run for 3–5 years, with a renewal option?
  Who pays for building repairs? Building maintenance?
  Are improvements and alterations permitted? Will the landlord pay for part of such costs?
  What does the rent include? Utilities? Garbage collection? Snow-clearing? Gardening services?
  Is an advance deposit or an extra month's rent required?
  Is 220-volt current for electrical equipment and 180° water for dishwashing available?
  What about customer parking and access rights?

- **From the Current Owner:**
  Why do you want to sell?
  How long have you owned this restaurant?
  Who owned it before you? Why did he sell?
  What has been your annual sales volume?
  Can you prove your figures? Through books of original entry? Through C.P.A. audits? Through your income tax statements?

What other records and books are available for inspection?

How much did you pay for the restaurant? Can you break this figure down for me?

Was it new when you bought it? What did you add?

Is the landlord cooperative? Reasonable? Fair-minded?

What about a liquor license? Can it be easily transferred?

What is the nature and extent of competition in the area?

Is the neighborhood changing? For the good or for the worse?

What changes, if any, would you advise me to make?

Are there any mortgages or other liens on your equipment, supplies, and other items of value?

Do you have any unpaid bills? How and when do you propose to pay them?

- **From Others (bankers, lawyers, vendors, restaurant equipment dealers, neighborhood businessmen, and accountants).**

  Why is the restaurant being sold?

  What is the verifiable volume of sales? What is the place really worth?

  What is happening to the neighborhood and community?

  Is the title to all assets free and clear?

  What is the present reputation of the restaurant?

  Is there a need for a new restaurant in the area? What kind?

  (From the banker): Are the existing mortgages transferable?

  What is the competition in the area?

Finally he bought a restaurant just outside of Norwalk from an elderly widower who wanted to retire.

Sam's business wasn't perfect. Much of the equipment had to be replaced, and the building had to be redecorated. But he did get a very good buy because he left no stone unturned.

If you are the brave type, you may discover that some of the best buys are restaurants that have failed miserably. The previous owner may have been totally inept at money management, even though the cook was superb and the customers loved the place. If the restaurant failed because of poor management, and you think you can do better, you may have discovered the bargain of your life. Some people like a challenge, too. The new owner may embark on a heavy advertising and promotional campaign to get the bad taste out of the mouths of the restaurant's old customers. As long as the location isn't horrible, the customers are not totally alienated, and the restaurant is in reasonably good condition, there is a good chance of making a go of it if you have an awful lot on the ball.

Another possibility is leasing a restaurant. There is a wide range of leasing situations. It is all between you and your landlord. The landlord may just rent a hole in a building and expect you to do all the finishing; on the other hand, the landlord may provide all the facilities. And there are two ways to pay: either a monthly rate or a percentage-of-sales lease. If the landlord provides all the equipment, a percentage lease will usually be drawn up. It is another drain on your profits, but it may be worth it to avoid the initial outlay of expenses for the equipment.

And finally, if you have the money and time, you may want to purchase a house or building and turn it into a restaurant. Again, if you check your paper you'll see several commercial properties claiming to be the perfect site for a restaurant. The arguments against this approach are almost as severe as building from scratch. There is the time spent redesigning and remodeling, the hassle with local zoning and building regulations, and the long time period it takes to get off the ground.

But if you do have the time, this approach can be extremely rewarding. Look at all the fine New England country inns and restaurants created from old homesteads. In one swoop they have preserved historic sites and chosen profitable themes for their food operations.

And it is possible to buy an old restaurant of one style and redo it in another style. One restaurant owner bought an old Chinese restaurant building that had been vacant for years. One reason that it had been vacant so long was that it was in the shape of a pagoda. Now what other use could that building be put to than either a Chinese restaurant or a Buddhist Temple? This clever owner turned it into a seafood restaurant. The pagoda points were trimmed, the roof was reshingled, round porthole windows were installed, and, after the paint job, the old temple had been transformed into a very attractive seafood restaurant with a shanty motif. It took many months, but it certainly was worthwhile, since he's been packing the patrons in and getting excellent reviews from local papers and magazines.

PICKING THE RIGHT LOCATION

There are more rules for picking the proper location than you can shake a lamb chop at. But location is more subtle than just picking out the proper population density. If success depended only on the amount of traffic that zipped by the restaurant's driveway, then all eateries would be on highways or in big cities along the main drag. Yet there are plenty of restaurants way out in the sticks, and they can be very lucrative. Does this mean that these restaurant owners chose their location on a whim? No, not at all. In Westchester County, a suburb of New York City, there are many successful "country" restaurants. Most are either gourmet or very high class. One establishment, the famous La Crémaillère, seems to be in a terrible spot. It is located in a tiny, ramshackle village about one hundred yards from a huge concrete warehouse that sells cut-rate vegetables and fire-sale items and about fifty yards from the local volunteer firehouse. Not a very impressive setting for one of the country's most gracious—and expensive— French restaurants. But hold on. Where do all those Rolls-Royces and Cadillacs come from? Well, it just so happens that the restaurant is smack between two of the richest communities in the country—Greenwich, Connecticut, and Bedford, New York. And the reputation of the restaurant is good enough to draw customers all the way from New York City to sample its fare. So while on the surface La Crémaillère's location seems terrible, in reality it couldn't be much better.

On the other hand, another restaurant about fifteen miles from La Crémaillère seemed to try the same strategy but wound up with opposite results. It had several different owners in a period of a couple years. All failed. The first couple of restaurants were steak houses, offering the usual salad bar, steak, and chicken fare. The setting was lovely. The restaurant was located in an old house and was done up in a pleasant Revolutionary War style. The food was fair to good, and the salad bar was one of the best in the county.

But the restaurant owners made several mistakes. The style of food service was not unusual enough to attract enough customers to its hideaway location. It was much too easy to miss.

It was in the middle of a residential area, and there were several private homes nearby.

What was even more confusing was the lack of a good sign. There was a tiny, unlit sign at the head of a common driveway with the restaurant and several private homes—but no sign at all at the restaurant itself. Since there were few cars, you couldn't be sure whether you had found the restaurant or somebody's home. The only clue was the enlarged driveway, but it wasn't big enough to clear away all doubts.

This restaurant and two similar ones in the same building closed. It is now in the hands of an owner who is trying his hand at private parties and catering in addition to regular lunch and dinner service.

Where does this leave you? It leaves you with the knowledge that you can't take any location for granted. La Crémaillère is a dignified French restaurant that thrives on its country-inn image. Its customers appreciate the food and the location. In all likelihood, if the owner had located it on a major highway and competed with truck stops, it would not have had a fraction of the success it has where it is. On the other hand, the steak-house owner, lacking a great reputation and offering rather ordinary food, probably would have been much more successful on the highway or in a city.

What can you do to make sure your location is correct for your establishment? It all boils down to a matter of compatibility: Is the location right for your restaurant and is your restaurant right for the location?

The best way to discover whether or not a location is good is with a proper analysis:

- Is it easy to get proper supplies?
- Do you like the area? Will you enjoy being where you are?
- How safe is the location? What chances are there that you will be robbed or vandalized?
- What is the future potential? Will there be growth or deterioration?
- Do you feel secure that you can make a good living in that spot?
- Will the community support another restaurant?

- Are there enough potential workers living within commuting distance of your restaurant?
- How do the zoning laws compare with others?
- What range of income does the average community resident have?
- How many competitors are there?
- How good is the waste-removal? The water system?
- How expensive are the utilities?

If your answers to the major personal and community questions satisfy you, then look at the plot of ground you plan to occupy in the near future.

- Are there proper parking facilities?
- Is there much traffic?
- Is the site in a good part of town?
- If you plan to locate on the highway, what are the chances that a new road will cut you off from the main path?
- Is it easy to find you? (If the directions are fifteen lefts, seven rights, six traffic lights, and an old oak tree, think twice.)
- How are your neighbors? (Don't try to locate a quiet intimate restaurant under a bowling alley or an elegant, high-class European-style restaurant next to a massage parlor.)

How do you find out all these facts? It's hard work. You have to be willing to talk to people—people such as employment agents, local officials, competitors, and business organizations. You have to dig in and discover whether or not the location you picked is good enough. If you want to open a cafeteria for breakfast and lunch, stand outside and see how many people walk or drive past in the morning and afternoon. Then try to find out where they go for breakfast and lunch. Don't open up next to a factory if the factory has its own commissary. If a nearby restaurant similar to the one you plan does a minimal business, how are two of you going to survive? On the other hand, if you see several restaurants lining up customers in the street, there certainly is room for you.

Don't get fooled by a lot of friends who keep saying this town really can use a good restaurant. Never take anything for granted. If you open without checking and rechecking every single factor that can affect your restaurant, you'll pay for it later. A little law about ventilation you didn't see or the fact that all those people in Podunk, Iowa, weren't really serious about needing an authentic Indonesian restaurant can close you down. Be careful. Watch out for the pitfalls, and you'll have a fair chance. The sad thing is that if you pick a real lemon of a site, you might spend over a year sinking money, effort, and time into a bottomless pit. It can break your heart.

BUYING EQUIPMENT

Buying equipment can be a real challenge. There are several methods. The easiest way is to find a reputable dealer and work with him. This becomes almost mandatory if you have to buy your equipment on time. A dealer will usually arrange financing with you.

But dealers and wholesalers aren't the only way. If you live near a large city, there may be auctions in your area. They are advertised in your local paper. For example:

Gavel Auction Co.

CLEAN UP-TO-DATE RESTAURANT

stainless steel equipment
2 Glenco self-contained refrigerator boxes
Garland 2 burner grill & broiler
Scotsman ice maker, Cold Spot freezer, SS salad box, steam table, coffee urn, work tables, soda fountain, milk dispenser, pots, pans, utensils, tables, chairs, servers, dishes, toasters, etc.

Bright Day Auction Co.

COMPLETE MODERN RESTAURANT
WITH EVERYTHING

Bar: 35′ oval padded bar, 15 bar stools, illuminated liquor display unit, modern refrigerator units, etc.

Dining room: 40 tables, 2, 4, 6 & 8 seaters with chairs, 10 booth units and 3 serving stations.

Kitchen—all stainless steel!: Billing counter, 8 salad carts, 3 door Toastmaster bread warmer, cold water dispenser, 12' combination sink & dish storage unit, globe slicer, Cory coffee grinder, AND MUCH, MUCH MORE! Including large quantity of dishes, glassware, pots, pans and utensils.

Often restaurants, both large and small, will just fold up and auction off all their wares. If you're lucky you can pick up excellent deals for a song. One warning: know what you're buying.

That rule applies to all your purchases. The cardinal rule is to purchase high-quality equipment *that you need*. Never go overboard and purchase deluxe material that you can't possibly use enough times to make it worth your while. A $1,500 expresso coffee machine is fine and dandy if you have a legitimate use for it. It is a complete waste if you sell just a couple of cups a night.

Restaurant equipment is expensive because it is heavy-duty—built to take a lot of punishment. But restaurant equipment is something like your family car, because there is an incredible rate of depreciation. Once you take the stuff out of the store and install it in your own restaurant, the value of the equipment immediately plummets. That's why you have to be careful when you purchase ovens, freezers, stoves, and other high-priced merchandise. If you sell it after a month of nonuse, you'll only get back a fraction of what you paid for it originally.

Before you buy anything—even napkins, plates, or glassware—do some comparison shopping. Maybe you can make a killing by haunting auctions and going-out-of-business sales. But you may discover that the best deal is from a wholesaler who'll give you a big break because you'll buy in quantity. You may even find out that it's best to buy a little here and a little there, some with cash and some on terms.

But no matter where you buy never forget: buy only what you need. Don't project your business years ahead when you purchase. It's best to wait until you have the business under control before you start expanding. Remember, these first few months and maybe even years are going to be tough. Before you're out of the woods you'll want every red cent back that you spent foolishly. Mistakes will be made, but try to avoid the big ones. Don't let anyone cheat or snow you, and don't snow yourself.

Do you know how much equipment you'll need? From estimates of business volume and knowledge of the type of operation you'll run, you can determine how much equipment you'll need and of what type. If you don't have a liquor license, don't buy those cases of wineglasses. Try to get away with the least amount possible. Of course, this doesn't mean that you can figure out to the exact glass or plate—you have to have a few replacements on hand for the inevitable breakage. But don't stock up on equipment. If what you purchase is never used, what good is it? Planning is the key again. Know what you want to buy and in what quantity.

FOURTEEN

You're Ready to Open

The Grand Opening / A Final Checklist

You've worked hard for months and you're ready to open your doors to admit the hungry hordes. Now is the time to stop and carefully recheck all that you've done. Are you really ready? You can't open those doors on a whim. Trying to build up a steady clientele without every single element of your operation geared to ready is like driving with a few drops of oil—the car will work beautifully while the oil lasts, but once it's gone, the car grinds to a halt.

THE GRAND OPENING

If you are planning to hold a grand opening, it is even more important that everything be just right. Bob Q. went all out to prepare for his restaurant's debut. He bought newspaper and magazine ads—some full-page—and he even did a few radio ads at the local station. This went on for two weeks before the opening. And he did a terrific job of promotion. The restaurant was covered with flags, and right about its roof was a big arrow pointing down with the caption: "This is the place." Well, it got so that the local people really were looking forward to the opening. And when the grand day came, they turned out by the carload.

At first Bob was ecstatic. Then he got the bad news. He was quickly running out of his introductory t-bone steak special, and his staff just wasn't handling the crowds well. What was worse was that the people were still lining up outside. Bob was getting desperate. His inexperienced staff was almost at a breaking point, and the specials at last were exhausted. Bob salvaged some of the disaster by giving everyone who wasn't able to buy the special a rain-check ticket with another healthy discount. This didn't stop the grumbling completely, but at least he didn't have a riot on his hands. For the next several months he had to work hard to erase the "success" of his grand opening.

You can see why many experts advise against having a grand opening—or at least to postpone it for a few weeks until the restaurant has had a good workout. But handled properly a grand opening can really help your restaurant. Bob Q. made no mistake in his approach to getting customers; he succeeded with flying colors. His real mistake was in poor preparation.

If you decide to have a grand opening, make sure that you:

- Have enough of everything—food, utensils, menus, napkins, ashtrays, etc.
- Have well-trained, prepared help. From cooks to waiters, everyone must know what to expect and be able to work under pressure. If you are planning for a huge number of opening-night guests, it may be worthwhile to hire some temporary workers.
- Have all equipment properly installed and working. Test everything from the ovens to the dishwasher. It would be disastrous if your opening-night special was a fish fry and you discovered that your fryer was broken.

Remember, opening night is for you to make a good impression on all your future customers. You want their business for years to come, so make everything just right. Good food, excellent service, pleasant surroundings have to be maintained. A mob of shouting, angry customers and a cowering group of sweaty waiters just won't help your image.

A FINAL CHECKLIST

Take some time and go over this checklist. Make sure you can answer yes to everything. Refer to Part I of this book and any other research source that offers you help on the subject.

- Have you set up a system of ordering food? Is it reliable?
- Do you have any alternative sources in case of an emergency?
- Have you learned how to order your food?
- Do you know how to purchase for the best quantity and quality?
- Are your storage facilities adequate?
- Is all your equipment installed and working properly?
- Is your menu all set? Have you planned future items?
- Are enough menus printed? Do they meet your standards?
- Do you have enough employees?
- Are you confident that your employees are well trained?
- Have you done your best to prevent pilfering?
- Have you met all local regulations?
- Is your operation sanitary?
- Do you have the proper insurance?
- Do you have an accounting system set up?
- Do you have an operating budget?
- Will you keep detailed records?
- Do you have the proper number of items—glassware, salt and pepper shakers, utensils, etc.?
- Do you have replacements?
- Have you advertised enough?
- Created any promotional gimmicks?
- Is your restaurant decorated to your satisfaction?
- Do you have a special theme or style?
- And the last, big question: do you feel confident about opening your restaurant at this time?

If you answered yes and have really prepared yourself, there's no reason you can't make it, and make it big. Good luck. Let's hope that in a few years your restaurant will be a national landmark.

INDEX